MAURICE BOWRA
a celebration

MAURICE BOWRA

a celebration

edited by
Hugh Lloyd-Jones

Duckworth

First published in 1974 by
Gerald Duckworth & Co Ltd
The Old Piano Factory
43 Gloucester Crescent, London NW1

ISBN 0 7156 0789 8

Printed in Great Britain by The Anchor Press Ltd,
and bound by Wm. Brendon & Son Ltd,
both of Tiptree, Essex

Contents

Books by Maurice Bowra

1928   *Pindar's Pythian Odes*, translated (with H. T. Wade-Gery). Nonesuch Press.

1930   *Oxford Book of Greek Verse*, edited (with Gilbert Murray, Cyril Bailey, E. A. Barber and T. F. Higham). Oxford.
Tradition and Design in the Iliad. Oxford.

1933   *Ancient Greek Literature*. Home University Library.

1935   *Pindari Carmina*. Oxford Classical Texts.

1936   *Greek Lyric Poetry* (2nd ed. 1961). Oxford.

1937   *Oxford Book of Greek Verse in Translation*, edited (with T. F. Higham). Oxford.

1938   *Early Greek Elegists*. Oxford.

1943   *The Heritage of Symbolism*. Macmillan.
A Book of Russian Verse. Oxford.

1944   *Sophoclean Tragedy*. Oxford.

1945   *From Virgil to Milton*. Macmillan.

1949   *The Creative Experiment*. Macmillan.

1950   *The Romantic Imagination*. Oxford.

1952   *Heroic Poetry*. Macmillan.

1953   *Problems in Greek Poetry*. Oxford.

1955   *Inspiration and Poetry*. Macmillan.

1957   *The Greek Experience*. Weidenfeld.

1962   *Primitive Song*. Weidenfeld.

1964   *In General and Particular*. Weidenfeld.
Pindar. Oxford.

1966   *Landmarks in Greek Literature*. Weidenfeld.
Poetry and Politics, 1900–1960. Cambridge.
Memories, 1898–1939. Weidenfeld.

1969   *The Odes of Pindar*, translated. Penguin.

1970   *On Greek Margins*. Oxford.

1971   *Periclean Athens*. Dial Press and Weidenfeld.

1972   *Homer*. Duckworth.

Preface

Five of the contributions to this volume, written soon after Maurice Bowra's death, have appeared in print before. I thank all those who have given permission for the reproduction of these contributions in this volume. Each is acknowledged at the appropriate place.

The remaining pieces have been written specially for this book, though it is likely that that of Mr. Powell will form part of an autobiography. In inviting people to contribute, I did not attempt to include all the closest friends of the subject, nor even to find contributors who would cover all his interests. The aim was to secure accounts of him by a sufficiently varied selection among those who knew him to give readers who did not an idea of the impressions which he made on those who did. Some account of his career as a scholar, writer and university administrator was necessary, and this will be found here. But what seemed most important was to record the personal impressions made by one whose writings and whose public achievements, notable as they were, seemed to those who knew him less important than the impact of his personality.

I am grateful to the *Oxford Mail* for the photograph which appears as frontispiece.

HUGH LLOYD-JONES

Christ Church, Oxford
2 July, 1974

I

The Times

A Brilliant Oxford Figure

Sir Maurice Bowra, C.H., Warden of Wadham College, Oxford, from 1938 to 1970, died yesterday. He was 73.

By his death Oxford has lost the most remarkable figure of his time in the university. A passionate interest in human beings, for themselves, for what they did and particularly for what they wrote, carried him from ancient China through classical antiquity, the Renaissance, Montparnasse and Russia to modernist poetry, and such was his literary sensitivity, his enthusiasm and above all his genius for communication, that generations of undergraduates and young dons have felt that they owed to him their first real grasp of the infinite variety of civilisation; so deep too was the impression he made that even the most critical have usually absorbed more than they realise of his outlook and of his style.

These were intensely original and catching, and, remarkably, they made their mark not on the second-rate but on men of independent genius. His influence can be detected on writers of such diverse gifts as Cyril Connolly, Rex Warner, C. Day Lewis, John Betjeman, Osbert Lancaster, Isaiah Berlin and A. J. Ayer, and there are others, such as Evelyn Waugh and Henry Green, who have owed something to his inspiration. But while this width of learning and sagacity are evident in his voluminous writings, his style on paper, though eminently orderly and lucid, tends to lack vitality and is quite unlike the scintillating, shimmering and sometimes thunderous wit of his conversation. Posterity will have no measure of his true greatness.

Nor will those who met him only in his later years when his short round figure had lost some of the bounce and energy that made it such an exciting part of the Oxford scene and when increasing deafness began to cut him off from those immediate contacts with strangers, especially the young, at which he had excelled.

* This obituary notice was published in *The Times* on 3 July 1971.

He was born on April 8, 1898, at Kiukiang on the Yangtse. His father, Cecil Arthur Vernon Bowra, was a Commissioner in the Chinese Customs Service, as his father had been before him. Vivid experience in the Far East in infancy and boyhood may have served to kindle his imagination. In 1903 he came to England but made further visits to the East in 1909 and again in 1916: on the way home that year he was held up in a Petrograd starving and on the edge of revolution; there he began his study of Russian.

He was at school at Cheltenham and was elected to a classical scholarship at New College in 1915. From September 1917 to the end of the First World War he served in France with the Royal Field Artillery; an experience which left him with no great love of the military and a profound and lasting loathing for war and the cruelty and stupidity that goes with it.

On going up to New College he at once became the acknowledged leader of a circle of exceptionally brilliant undergraduates among whom only one, J. B. S. Haldane, could rival his range and none his wit and fluency. He was already enormously well read; Anatole France, whose wide range may have served as a model, was a favourite with him just then. And already in his freshman days he was as fully armed as he ever became with his gifts of swift epigram and verbal ingenuity. Of his tutors Alick Smith (later Warden Smith) won him by his humanity and was in many ways his model as tutor, Dean and Warden: while Gilbert Murray's sense of style and attitude to scholarship, so Bowra himself claimed, shaped his whole academic life.

After obtaining firsts in Classical Moderations and Greats, he became in 1922 classical tutor and Fellow of Wadham. At various times he was Dean and Senior Tutor, and in 1930–1 was appointed Proctor. His boundless hospitality made Wadham in those days the most familiar of all Oxford colleges to many Londoners: a hospitality memorable above all for his special brand of conversation. In developing a theme, whether about men or books, he would push on to extremes of exaggeration and, sometimes, fantasy, which might appear hilariously funny at the time only for the verbal and imaginative dexterity but which depended for their real effect on an originality and an element of truth that gave an edge to all he said and which only a very few great 'wits' command.

But the social side of his life, while important to him and to the many who shared it, absorbed only a tiny part of his energies. He was intensely proud of his college and devoted himself to its affairs, not only in the business of administration but by entering into easy friendly relations with undergraduates, and by working hard to raise its intellectual standards. At the early age of 40 he was elected Warden (in 1938). During the war little could be done for the college but he faced the problem of returning ex-servicemen in 1945 with characteristic foresight and radicalism. He filled what had been a small college to bursting-point, some said beyond it, and then moved on at once to deal with the consequences; to build up the teaching strength, to increase accommodation for undergraduates, to answer the new demands of the sciences, above all to turn quantity into quality. An additional Fellow, an extra room, another First, nothing pleased him more, and the improvement he achieved in the intellectual standing of the college and in its buildings, which during his time as Warden were renovated and much extended, is the memorial he would most have valued.

In all this he was supported by devoted colleagues, but it was Bowra who gave the impetus and the optimism that made it possible to succeed. More than that, his own experience during and after the First World War, together with his natural humanity, helped him to understand the problems of this generation and to solve them as humanely as Alick Smith had solved those of Bowra's own undergraduate days. Clever and less-clever alike had their faith in civilised life restored by his sympathy, generosity, excitement, wit and, when needed, anger. His response to the special problems of later generations of undergraduates was less spontaneous but on any matter of principle unerringly right. When, for example, in 1968 some undergraduates wanted to have their objections to the proctorial system heard by the Privy Council, Bowra was the first to give them public support, and in answer to the objection 'Why should they?' answered simply 'Because they are entitled to and because they want to.' More and more demands were made on his time, by the university, by other universities and institutions in the United Kingdom and abroad (he played a conspicuous part in the foundation of the British Institute in Teheran in 1962), by friends and admirers, academic and literary, throughout the world, and to all these he gave lavishly; but none of them ever took precedence over the claims of Wadham's humblest under-graduate or youngest don.

In 1951–4 Bowra was Vice-Chancellor. For many years both before and after this he did full service on the various important bodies of the university – the Hebdomadal Council, Chest, General Board and Clarendon Press.

He was an efficient administrator; his power of swift thought enabled him to polish off business quickly. In the chair he was staccato and relevant; he brought in his fun and jokes in modera-tion and he made everyone feel lively. As vice-chancellor he prided himself in taking special trouble with new appointments, and, whatever the extra demands on him, he greatly raised the standard of hospitality and consideration shown to honorands and other distinguished visitors to Oxford, to many of whom he became, if he was not already, the university's most distinguished name. More important, in the university, as already in his college, he was trying to face, not always successfully, those problems of growth, finance, administration and admissions which were not generally recognised for a decade or more.

Bowra's extraordinary powers of concentration were such that he never let this other work interfere with his studies or the copious flow of his writings. Most of these are concerned with literary criticism. Though not a great critic he had two impor-tant assets: an unerring eye for the best in literature, and an ability to communicate his enthusiasm for it. He reached a wide circle of readers, and there can be few of them whose horizons have not been in some way enlarged by his books.

In his classical writings, as in his lecturing, his aim, like that of his master, Murray, was to keep the Greeks alive; and though his style was not such a delicate instrument as Murray's, his grasp of the Greek mind was more direct and realistic, and found a ready response in the audience for which he wrote, namely the generations which came after the First World War. His *Ancient Greek Literature* (1933), an excellent short survey, *The Oxford Book of Greek Verse in Translation* (1937), of which he was the editor, and which contained many of his own verse translations, *The Greek Experience* (1957), perhaps the best book of its kind yet written, and *Landmarks in Greek Literature* (1966), aimed at diffusing knowledge and understanding of the Greek world to a wide public; much earlier he collaborated with H. T. Wade-Gery, a friend and colleague whose stimulating influence can be seen in some of his best work, in a translation of Pindar's *Pythian Odes* (1928), which deserves to be more widely known.

His more specialised works of scholarship are somewhat unequal. *Early Greek Elegists* (1938) is a slight though useful introduction; *Sophoclean Tragedy* (1944) lacks his customary insight; and his edition of the text of Pindar (1935) has now been superseded. But *Tradition and Design in the Iliad* (1930) and *Greek Lyric Poetry*, in its revised form (1961: first edition 1936), are lasting contributions to classical studies; and above all his book on Pindar (1964) is a masterly performance, rivalling the standard work of Wilamowitz. Besides these, Bowra wrote many valuable articles, the most important up to 1953 being collected in *Problems in Greek Poetry*; and it is in this smaller compass that he did some of his best work.

He was always at pains to see literature in the context of the society in which it was written; his main concern was with ideas rather than words. He despised perfectionism and pedantry alike as forms of laziness, wasting on minutiae time better spent on grappling with larger tasks; and he never paraded his knowledge of secondary literature. This sometimes led to errors and omissions in his work; but it also led critics to underestimate his scholarship, learning and originality.

His specifically classical interests, however, accounted for only a part of his output. In *The Heritage of Symbolism* (1943) he showed his skill in the interpretation of modern poets. In a similar field was *The Creative Experiment* (1949), on which Pasternak commented that it was the best interpretation of him that he had seen. (In 1943 he had already published his *Book of Russian Verse* including more of his own verse translations.) On the earlier masters he wrote *From Virgil to Milton* (1945), *The Romantic Imagination* (1949) and *Heroic Poetry* (1952); the last was heroic in another sense – its range was probably beyond the capacity of any other living scholar. In 1955 he published *Inspiration and Poetry* and in 1962 a remarkable work, *Primitive Song*, a study of oral poetry surviving in Africa and elsewhere.

But here too some of his best work was on a smaller scale: *In General and Particular* (1964) is a selection of these shorter essays which includes some of the outstanding lectures which he gave in Oxford and elsewhere, 'The Meaning of a Heroic Age' (Earl Grey

Lecture, Newcastle 1957) and 'Poetry and the First World War' (Taylorian Lecture, Oxford 1963). In 1966 he published his *Memories*, a deliberately selective account of his own life up to 1938 and of the people he knew. In this book he appropriately shed the stiffness of his more formal writing and conveyed something of the tones which made his conversation memorable: and though it is not uniformly successful – least, perhaps, in its set-piece character-sketches – it reveals its author's observation and humanity as well as his wit. *On Greek Margins* was published in 1970.

Bowra became an Honorary Fellow of Wadham College and an Honorary D.C.L. of Oxford University in 1970. *Periclean Athens*, his last book published in his lifetime, appeared this year.

His services to scholarship were widely recognised. He was awarded the Conington Prize at Oxford in 1930, was made a Doctor of Letters in 1937 and from 1946 to 1951 was Professor of Poetry. He became a member of the British Academy in 1938 and from 1958 to 1962 was its President. He was awarded honorary doctorates by Trinity College, Dublin, and by the Universities of Wales, Hull, St Andrews, Paris, Aix-en-Provence, Columbia and Harvard where he also gave the Charles Eliot Norton lectures on poetry in 1948–9. He was knighted in 1951, was a Commandeur de la Légion d'Honneur and a Knight-Commander of the Greek Royal Order of the Phoenix.

To the outsider he could appear a formidable and sometimes unsympathetic figure, disturbingly frank and non-conformist to the old (he was a free-thinker, an epicure and an uninhibited advocate of pleasure), determinedly old-fashioned to the young. He was also extremely sensitive to criticism, especially when it came from someone on whose loyalty he relied, and in his younger days there were periods of estrangement even from his best friends.

But at his most wrathful – and no one then could rival his verve and wit in denigration – he was careful to say nothing that would really damage a friend, and those who knew him well were absolutely confident of his generosity and rock-like loyalty. They also knew that the old were usually shocked because they themselves were not flexible enough to keep up with him and that the young were puzzled because they could not see through the manners of a past generation to the real Bowra.

He was a young radical who stayed both young and radical to

the end; that he always tended to the Left in politics, the non-professional Left, was only one accidental result of this extraordinary ability to keep abreast of the modern world. He saw through new pomposities, pretensions and hypocrisies as he had seen through the old, and was devastating in his invective against them, but his mind was always open to new ideas of value and they could find no more energetic or eloquent advocate. Above all he was throughout a passionate apostle of toleration and hated cruelty and injustice in any form; nor did he stop at words in helping their victims at home and abroad.

Older friends of Bowra could see in him an emblem of the survival of civilised values; younger friends (and difference of age was never any bar to real friendship) learnt from him to distinguish what was really valuable from what was merely prejudice. It was not his erudition, it was not even his wit, that was the secret of his influence. It was his deep-rooted and passionate belief in certain attributes of civilisation, in the comfortable life, in the value of art and of the pursuit of truth, and, most of all, in human freedom. On these central issues he was adamantine. Some have seen in Bowra a man of action *manqué*, whose energies and talents called for a wider sphere than the academic world to which he confined them. But for all his strength and shrewdness, he lacked the qualities of ruthlessness and calculation which go with the pursuit and exercise of power; and this lack made him greater as a human being than many men of his time who possessed them.

2

Isaiah Berlin

Memorial Address in St Mary's

We are here to commemorate the life of Maurice Bowra, our friend and colleague; scholar, critic, and administrator, the greatest English wit of his day; but, above all, a generous and warm-hearted man, whose powerful personality transformed the lives and outlook of many who came under his wide and life-giving influence. According to a contemporary at Cheltenham, he was fully formed by the time he left school for the army in 1916. In firmness of character he resembled his father, of whom he always spoke with deep affection and respect; but unlike him he was rebellious by temperament and, when he came up to New College in 1919, became the natural leader of a group of intellectually gifted contemporaries, passionately opposed to the conventional wisdom and moral code of those who formed pre-war Oxford opinion. He remained critical of all establishments for ever after. Bowra loved life in all its manifestations. He loved the sun, the sea, warmth, light, and hated cold and darkness, physical, intellectual, moral, political. All his life he liked freedom, individuality, independence, and detested everything that seemed to him to cramp and constrict the forces of human vitality, no matter what spiritual achievements such self-mortifying asceticism might have to its credit. His passion for the Mediterranean and its cultures was of a piece with this : he loved pleasure, exuberance, the richest fruits of nature and civilisation, the fullest expression of human feeling, uninhibited by a Manichean sense of guilt. Consequently he had little sympathy for those who recoiled from the forces of life – cautious, calculating conformists, or those who seemed to him prigs or prudes who winced at high vitality or passion, and were too easily shocked by vehemence and candour. Hence his impatience with philistine majorities in the academic and official and com-

* Delivered in the University Church of St Mary the Virgin, Oxford, on 17 July 1971.

mercial worlds, and equally with cultural coteries which appeared
to him thin, or old-maidish, or disapproving. He believed in
fullness of life. Romantic exaggeration, such as he found in the
early thirties in the circle formed round the German poet Stefan
George, appealed to him far more than British reticence. With
a temperament that resembled men of an older generation – Win-
ston Churchill or Thomas Beecham – he admired genius, splendour,
eloquence, the grand style, and had no fear of orchestral colour;
the chamber music of Bloomsbury was not for him. He found his
ideal vision in the classical world: the Greeks were his first and
last love. His first and best book was a study of Homer; this, too,
was the topic of his last book, had he lived to complete it.[1] Despite
the vast sweep of his literary interests – from the epic songs of
Central Africa to the youngest poet of our day – it is Pindar,
Sophocles, the Greek lyric poets who engaged his deepest feelings.
Murray and Wilamowitz meant more to him than scholars and
critics of other literatures.

Endowed with a sharp, quick brain, a masterful personality,
an impulsive heart, great gaiety, a brilliant, ironical wit, contempt
for all that was solemn, pompous, and craven, he soon came to
dominate his circle of friends and acquaintances. Yet he suffered
all his life from a certain lack of confidence: he needed constant
reassurance. His disciplined habits, his belief in, and capacity for,
hard, methodical work in which much of his day was spent, his
respect for professionalism and distaste for dilettantism, all these
seemed, in some measure, defensive weapons against ultimate self-
distrust. So, indeed, was his Byronic irony about the very Romantic
values that were closest to his heart. The treatment of him at New
College by that stern trainer of philosophers, H. W. B. Joseph,
undermined his faith in his own intellectual capacity, which his
other tutor in Philosophy, Alick Smith, who did much for him, and
became a lifelong friend, could not wholly restore.

Bowra saw life as a series of hurdles, a succession of fences to
take: there were books, articles, reviews to write; pupils to teach,
lectures to deliver; committees, even social occasions, were so
many challenges to be met, no less so than the real ordeals –
attacks by hostile critics, or vicissitudes of personal relationships,

---

[1] Nine out of ten chapters were later found, and the book was published
in 1972. (Ed.)

B

or the hazards of health. In the company of a few familiar friends, on whose loyalty he could rely, he relaxed and often was easy, gentle, and at peace. But the outer world was full of obstacles to be taken at a run; at times he stumbled, and was wounded: he took such reverses with a stiff upper lip; and then, at once, energetically moved forward to the next task. Hence, it may be, his need and craving for recognition, and the corresponding pleasure he took in the many honours he received. The flat, pedestrian, lucid, well-ordered, but, at times, conventional style and content of his published writings, may also be due to this peculiar lack of faith in his own true and splendid gifts. His private letters, his private verse, and above all his conversation, were a very different matter. Those who know him solely through his published works can have no inkling of his genius.

As a talker he could be incomparable. His wit was verbal and cumulative: the words came in short, sharp bursts of precisely aimed, concentrated fire, as image, pun, metaphor, parody, seemed spontaneously to generate one another in a succession of marvellously imaginative patterns, sometimes rising to high, wildly comical, fantasy. His unique accent, idiom, voice, the structure of his sentences, became a magnetic model which affected the style of speech, writing, and perhaps feeling, of many who came under its spell. It had a marked effect on some among the best known Oxford-bred writers of our time. But his influence went deeper than this: he dared to say things which others thought or felt, but were prevented from uttering by rules or convention or personal inhibitions. Maurice Bowra broke through some of these social and psychological barriers, and the young men who gathered round him in the twenties and thirties, stimulated by his unrestrained talk, let themselves go in their turn. Bowra was a major liberating force: the free range of his talk about art, personalities, poetry, civilisations, private life, his disregard of accepted rules, his passionate praise of friends and unbridled denunciation of enemies, produced an intoxicating effect. Some eyebrows were raised, especially among the older dons, at the dangers of such licence. They were wholly mistaken. The result, no matter how frivolous the content, was deeply and permanently emancipating. It blew up much that was false, pretentious, absurd; the effect was cathartic; it made for truth, human feeling, as well as great mental exhilaration. The host (and he was always host, whether in his own rooms or those of others) was a positive personality; his character was cast in a major key: there was nothing corrosive or decadent or embittered in all this talk, no matter how irreverent or indiscreet or extravagant or unconcerned with justice it was.

As a scholar, and especially as a critic, Bowra had his limitations. His most valuable quality was his deep and unquenchable love of literature, in particular of poetry, of all periods and peoples. His travels in Russia before the Revolution, when as a schoolboy he crossed that country on his way to his family's home in China, gave him a life-long interest in Russian poetry. He learnt Russian as a literary language, and virtually alone in England happily (and successfully) parsed the obscurest lines of modern Russian poets as he did the verse of Pindar or Alcaeus. He read French, German, Italian, and Spanish, and had a sense of world literature as a single firmament, studded with works of genius the quality of which he laboured to communicate. He was one of the very few Englishmen equally well known to, and valued by, Pasternak and Quasimodo, Neruda, and Seferis, and took proper pride in this. It was all, for him, part of the war against embattled philistinism, pedantic learning, parochialism. Yet he was, with all this, a stout-hearted patriot, as anyone could testify who heard him in Boston, for example, when England was even mildly criticised. Consequently, the fact that no post in the public service was offered him in the Second World War distressed him. He was disappointed, too, when he was not appointed to the Chair of Greek at Oxford (he was offered chairs by Harvard and other distinguished universities). But later he came to look on this as a blessing in disguise; for his election as Warden of Wadham eventually made up and more than made up for it all.

Loyalty was the quality which, perhaps, he most admired, and one with which he was himself richly endowed. His devotion to Oxford, and in particular to Wadham, sustained him during the second, less worldly, portion of his life. He did a very great deal for his college, and it did much for him. He was intensely and, indeed, fiercely proud of Wadham, and of all its inhabitants, senior and junior; he seemed to be on excellent terms with every undergraduate in its rapidly expanding population; he guided them and helped them, and performed many acts of kindness by stealth. In his last decades he was happiest in his Common Room, or when entertaining colleagues or undergraduates; happiest of all, when surrounded by friends, old or young, on whose love and loyalty he could depend. After Wadham his greatest love was for the University: he served it faithfully as proctor, member of the Hebdomadal Council, and of many other committees, as Delegate of the Press, finally as Vice-Chancellor. Suspected in his younger days of being a cynical epicure (no less cynical man ever breathed), he came to be respected as one of the most devoted, effective, and progressive of academic statesmen. He had a very strong institutional sense: his presidency of the British Academy was a very happy period of his life. Under his enlightened leadership the Academy prospered. But it was Oxford that claimed his deeper allegiance: the progress of the University filled him with intense and lasting pride. Oxford and Wadham were his home and his life; his soul was bound up with both. Of the many honours which he received, the honorary doctorate of his own University gave him the deepest satisfaction: the opinion of his colleagues was all in all to him. When the time for retirement came, he was deeply grateful to his college for making it possible for him to continue to live within its walls. His successor was an old personal friend: he felt sure of affection and attention.

Increasing ill health and deafness cut him off from many pleasures, chief among them committees and the day-to-day business of administration which he missed as much as the now less accessible pleasures of social life. Yet his courage, his gaiety, his determination to make the most of what opportunities remained, did not desert him. His sense of the ridiculous was still acute; his sense of fantasy remained a mainstay. New faces continued to feed his appetite for life. Most of all he now enjoyed his contact with the young, whose minds and hearts he understood, and whose desire to resist authority and the imposition of frustrating rules he instinctively shared and boldly supported to the end. They felt this and responded to him, and this made him happy.

He was not politically-minded. But by temperament he was a radical and a non-conformist. He genuinely loathed reactionary views and had neither liking nor respect for the solid pillars of any establishment. He sympathised with the unions in the General Strike of 1926; he spoke with passion at an Oxford meeting against the suppression of Socialists in Vienna by Dollfuss in 1934; he detested oppression and repression, whether by the Right or Left, and in particular all dictators. His friendship with Hugh

Gaitskell was a source of pleasure to him. If political sentiments which seemed to him retrograde or disreputable were uttered in his presence, he was not silent and showed his anger. He did not enjoy the altercations to which this tended to lead, but would have felt it shameful to run away from them; he possessed a high degree of civil courage. He supported all libertarian causes, particularly minorities seeking freedom or independence, the more unpopular, the better. Amongst his chief pleasures in the late fifties and sixties were the Hellenic cruises in which he took part every year. But when the present regime in Greece took over, he gave them up.

His attitude to religion was more complicated and obscure: he had a feeling for religious experience; he had no sympathy for positivist or materialist creeds. But to try to summarise his spiritual outlook in a phrase would be absurd as well as arrogant. As Warden he is said scarcely ever to have missed Chapel.

The last evening of his life was spent at a convivial party with colleagues and undergraduates. This may have hastened the heart attack of which he died; if so, it was as he would have wished it to be: he wanted to end swiftly and tidily, as he had lived, before life had become a painful burden.

He was, in his prime, the most discussed Oxford personality since Jowett, and in every way no less remarkable and no less memorable.

3

Hugh Lloyd-Jones

British Academy Memoir

Cecil Maurice Bowra was born on 8 April 1898 at Kiukiang, in China, where his father, Cecil Arthur Verner Bowra, of a Kentish family, was working as an official in the Chinese Customs Service. His father was an intelligent and cultivated person, conservative in his opinions and somewhat austere in character, who combined loyalty to his own country with devotion to the interests of his Chinese employers. During his childhood Maurice Bowra was somewhat in awe of his father, but later they could talk without reserve. Maurice was clearly more like his father's father, Edward Charles Bowra, also a Chinese scholar and a member of the Customs Service, a dashing and imaginative person who unfortunately died young. Cecil Bowra was brought up by his mother, daughter of an East India Company official, Samuel Woodward, by a natural daughter of the Lord Cornwallis who was Viceroy. This is why Maurice Bowra was able to reply to an inquiry whether his family had any connection with the United States by saying, 'Not since my great-great-grandfather surrendered at Yorktown.' In childhood Maurice Bowra saw less of his father than of his mother, born Ethel Lovibond, the daughter of a brewer living in Fulham, who though a collateral descendant of John Locke preferred to claim descent from the last man in England hanged for forgery. She was a gay and amusing person with a special gift for understanding others, even if their background was very different from her own.

Soon after Maurice Bowra's birth his father was transferred to Newchwang, in Manchuria, and he spent happy early years there before being brought to England in 1905. Living with his paternal grandmother and her second husband, the Revd George Mackie, at Putney, he first had lessons from a governess – Ethel M. Dell's

---

* Originally published in *Proceedings of the British Academy* 58, 1972, 393 ff.

sister – and then went to an old-fashioned but good boarding school kept by two ladies. Here, with lessons from Cecil Botting, a master at St Paul's who collaborated with his High Master in the well-known Greek textbook known as 'Hillard and Botting', he began his classical education.

After an exciting visit to his parents, now at Mukden in Man-churia, in 1909–10, Bowra at the age of twelve entered Chelten-ham College. The place and its headmaster, the Revd Reginald Waterfield, were not free from the absurdities of the Victorian school, as Bowra was well able to appreciate. But it provided a sound training in Greek and Latin; G. F. Exton, a dry Cambridge scholar, gave a good grammatical grounding, and Leonard Butler, later a Fellow of St John's College, Oxford, gave Bowra a taste for writing Greek verse which he carried into later life. But Bowra found the school work boring, and used his last two years in the sixth form not to concentrate on classics, but to read widely. He learned French well enough to understand Ver-laine and Baudelaire, tackled the Divine Comedy in a bilingual edition, and began to learn German. In 1916 he won the top scholarship to New College, Oxford.

Soon after this he returned to China by the Trans-Siberian Railway to spend the interval before joining the army in a visit to his parents. This journey, made at the most impressionable age, was of great importance in his life. He was deeply impressed by the marvels of Peking, where his father was now living as Chief Secretary of the Customs Service with an establishment of thirty servants and a cook who bore the title of 'Great Eating Professor'. On the way back he had the great good fortune to stay for some time in Petrograd. He made friends who were able to inform him about the interesting state of Russia at that time, and quickly acquired a working knowledge of the language. He was deeply fascinated by a brilliant and delightful Russian girl, who, he later wrote, 'had much fancy and humour, and unlike some Russians did not bother to talk about her soul or even mine'. This girl afterwards disappeared during the Revolution, and may have starved to death. To the end of his life Bowra wrote and spoke of her as he did of no other person, and it is clear that she filled a special place in his affection.

Bowra kept the Michaelmas Term of 1916 in a depleted Oxford; but early in 1917 he joined the Royal Field Artillery. He trained at an officer cadet school in Bloomsbury, and was much irritated by the 'spit and polish' on which his instructors insisted; but he made good friends, and managed to complete the course successfully. In September he was commissioned, and went to France in time to take part in the later stages of the Third Battle of Ypres. Later he was present at the successful action at Cambrai, and saw much heavy fighting during Ludendorff's offensive of March 1918 and the decisive counter-offensive of the month of August.

'Whatever you hear about the war,' Bowra later said to Cyril Connolly,[1] 'remember it was inconceivably bloody – nobody who wasn't there can ever imagine what it was like.' But he carried out his duties with success, and seems to have developed at this time the ability to get on terms with very different people that he showed later. While in the trenches he read widely. He read a good deal of modern literature – during one leave he bought together Hardy's *Moments of Vision*, Yeats's *The Wild Swans at Coole*, and Eliot's *Prufrock*; but he read also Greek and Latin books, which now that he had left Cheltenham he took up with keen interest.

In April 1919, Bowra came into residence at New College, and from then until his death Oxford was his home. The cultural break occasioned by the First World War did not take effect immediately; it was not until the thirties, after the slump, that the wet blanket of collectivist thinking came down to stifle English intellectual life. The Oxford of the twenties contained many people who were not only intelligent but also gay and amusing, and in this society Bowra's quick wit and dominating personality made him conspicuous. Bowra's undergraduate friends in his own college included, to name only those who later became famous, Cyril Radcliffe, Roy Harrod, and Henry Price, and J. B. S. Haldane was a young don there; in other colleges he met Robert Boothby, L. P. Hartley, and Lord David Cecil; he frequented the *salons*, if that is the right word, of F. F. Urquhart and R. H. Dundas, and in Cambridge got to know G. H. W. Rylands.

At this time and for long afterwards Bowra presented a formidable as well as an engaging figure. 'I was not nearly so sure of myself as I should have liked,' he later wrote, 'and this made me present a brassy face to the world and pretend to be more hard-

[1] See p. 44.

boiled than I was.' Like most people with the wit to think of them, he found it hard to resist the temptation to utter devastating remarks; and the temptation was strengthened by the extreme sensitivity which never left him. One can understand the rumour that the character of Markie Linkwater in his friend Elizabeth Bowen's novel *To the North* owed something to the impression made by the young Bowra.

New College at that time cannot be said to have offered the best classical tuition to be had in Oxford. The Mods tutor was the flaccid and unappealing H. L. Henderson, and the Greats historian, P. E. Matheson, was then well past a not very impressive best. One philosophy tutor was A. H. Smith, a cultivated and sympathetic person who did all he could to help Bowra and was to remain his friend for life; but Smith was scarcely the man to give him the intellectual training which he needed. The other tutor in philosophy was H. W. B. Joseph, who devoted great force of will and not inconsiderable ability to the rigorous enforcement of his own brand of dogmatic idealism upon his pupils. It is hard to imagine a tutor less congenial to Bowra than this chilly scholastic, who in Sir Isaiah Berlin's opinion 'undermined his faith in his own intellectual capacity'.[1]

Fortunately not all the tuition Bowra received was from the Fellows of his own college. Gilbert Murray had been Regius Professor of Greek since 1908, but still contrived to give some personal instruction to undergraduates, and this together with his lectures was far more important to Bowra than anything his other tutors could provide. Bowra wrote with special appreciation of Murray's famous classes in the translation into Greek of English verse and prose. Bowra was at all times a strong believer in the educational value of this now unfairly disparaged and neglected exercise, particularly in the hands of a scholar like Murray or J. D. Denniston. Bowra did not win any of the university scholarships and prizes given primarily for composition and in those days highly valued; but he obtained First Classes both in Mods and Greats.

In 1922 Bowra, with the support of Murray and his old friend A. S. Owen of Keble, was elected to a tutorial fellowship at Wadham College, at that time, despite the beauty of its buildings and the eminence of some of its old members, a small, poor and

[1] See p. 17.

not notably distinguished institution. In later years his tuition was
sometimes a little hasty; but it was always exciting, and in his early
years it was superb. Wadham did not provide Bowra with the
most promising material, but he had among his pupils a future
Secretary of the Cabinet in Norman Brook, a future historian of
the Delphic Oracle in H. W. Parke, and a future Poet Laureate in
Cecil Day Lewis. He also took an effective part in college business,
being prominent among those who placed the finances of Wadham
on a new footing by persuading the governing body to sell part
of the Warden's garden to allow the building of Rhodes House.
In 1930 he was elected to serve as Proctor, thus gaining the best
possible introduction to the business of the university.

Bowra's social life as a young don was even more varied and
exciting than it had been while he was an undergraduate. He more
than anyone helped to launch into civilised life the brilliant generation that came up after the immediate postwar years, and aesthetes
like Brian Howard and Harold Acton, scholars like Kenneth
Clark, Isaiah Berlin, Roger Mynors and John Sparrow, and men of
letters like John Betjeman, Cyril Connolly, 'Henry Green' and
Evelyn Waugh all owed much to his friendship and his influence.
At that time several houses in the neighbourhood of Oxford were
centres of intellectual activity, and Bowra was at home in all of
them; he visited the Murrays on Boar's Hill, the Morrells at
Garsington, and the Asquiths at Sutton Courtney, and made
contact with other distinguished frequenters of these establishments.

Bowra spent part of his vacations in continental travel, and
like other English intellectuals during the twenties and early
thirties he found Weimar Germany a fascinating study. A visit on
the way back from Yugoslavia with Hugh Gaitskell in 1927 was
followed by a longer stay in 1932, when his friend Adrian Bishop
was living in Berlin. He became intimate with several distinguished Germans, notably with the historian Ernst Kantorowicz,
with the Curator of the University of Frankfurt, Kurt Riezler, and
his wife, and with Baroness Lucy von Wangenheim. All these had
some connection with the circle about Stefan George, of whom
Bowra later wrote in *The Creative Experiment*; the classical
scholar closest to this group was Karl Reinhardt, whom Bowra
much admired. His visits to Germany enabled Bowra to form an
early first-hand impression of the National Socialists, for whom,

unlike many English people at that time, he conceived and expressed an instant disgust.

Even while his social life and college employments were at their height, Bowra was never idle. The habit of reading in bed, which he maintained throughout his life, ensured that he continued to extend his knowledge; and what he read he usually remembered. An article on 'Homeric Words in Arcadian Inscriptions' (*Classical Quarterly* 20, 1926, 168 ff., followed up in 'Homeric Words in Cyprus', *Journal of Hellenic Studies* 54, 1934, 54 ff.) was a pioneer work; later the decipherment of Linear B was to lend special interest to these investigations of the two Greek dialects that conserved most Mycenaean features. In 1928 he published, in collaboration with his Wadham colleague H. T. Wade-Gery, a translation of Pindar's *Pythian Odes* into free verse, which was beautifully printed by the Nonesuch Press. This was one of the first renderings of Greek verse – certainly one of the first by academic persons – to throw off the worn-out trappings of sub-Tennysonian traditionalist verse. It had a deserved success, and later formed the basis of the translation of all Pindar's epinician odes which Bowra published in the Penguin Classics series in 1969. More good translations by Bowra have appeared in *The Oxford Book of Greek Verse in Translation* (1938).

In 1930 Bowra published *Tradition and Design in the Iliad*, a well-written and well-reasoned book which ranks high among his writings. He was not the only scholar at that time to maintain that 'there was a single poet called Homer, who gave the *Iliad* its final shape and artistic unity, but who worked in a traditional style on traditional matter'. But Bowra's book is wholly free from the nationalism and sentimentality that disfigured other unitarian studies in the English language. It gets to grips with the central problems of composition, but is not afraid to describe and discuss the *Iliad* as we have it as a poem with a plot and with its own kind of unity, and he never loses himself in mists of archaeological and linguistic detail. Bowra was acquainted with the work of Murko, though not yet with that of Milman Parry, whose *L'Epithète Traditionnelle* had appeared two years before, and at one point considered whether the *Iliad* might not be an oral poem. He concludes that Homer is likelier than not to have used writing, but to have used it for his own use, not for the poem to be read, but for it to be recited; we shall see presently how interesting it is, in the light of current opinion, to find this in a book published as long ago as 1930. The work has a freshness and liveliness that make it after more than forty years still well worth reading.

During the thirties Bowra was mainly occupied with early Greek lyric poetry. Papyrus publications had substantially increased the small amount of material available, and elucidation was badly needed. With Wade-Gery as his colleague in Wadham Bowra kept in close touch with the latest developments in early Greek history, archaeology, and art, and set out to use this to illuminate the poetry.

Bowra was not suited to be a textual critic. He lacked the accuracy and caution expected of an editor, and he had been denied the gift of textual divination. The presentation of the early lyric poems in *The Oxford Book of Greek Verse* (1930), for which he was responsible, leaves much to be desired; and his Oxford text of Pindar (1935), though its apparatus criticus contains some useful matter, has not enough positive merits to compensate for its numerous inaccuracies. In 1936 he brought out *Greek Lyric Poetry*, a large interpretative book which devotes a chapter to each major figure; in 1938 it was followed by *Early Greek Elegists*, a slighter volume which contained Martin Lectures delivered at Oberlin College in Ohio. In later years Bowra was critical of the former book, which in 1961 he subjected to a radical revision.

'I was too often carried away by my imagination [he wrote] and did not pay a sufficiently critical attention to views which I put forward because they fascinated me. Nor was I careful enough with some small details. I knew that they mattered and I enjoyed discoursing about them, but with them too enthusiasm was not enough. In trying to find solutions for all problems I went further than the fragmentary evidence allowed, and too many of my hypotheses were fragmentary and unsubstantiated.'

That characteristically severe self-criticism is just; but the book's failings are not only on the side of technical scholarship. The writing slides far too easily into cliché; people who knew Bowra only from his conversation must have been staggered to find him capable of writing 'Alcman well understood the Spartan girls who sang in his choirs and entered completely into their happy dainty longings' or 'Over their ripening desires Sappho presided'. Correspondingly, the critical approach adopted to the authors is disappointingly conventional. Yet with all its faults the book has attractive qualities, showing as it does its author's wide knowledge and real love of literature. To a beginner in scholarship at that time it seemed to offer a fascinating glimpse of the picture of early Greek civilisation then being drawn, under the influence of Beazley, by men like Payne and Blakeway, and to help the reader to enjoy the precious fragments whose number the papyri had excitingly increased.

In 1936 the Regius Chair of Greek at Oxford was to be vacated by the retirement of Gilbert Murray, to whom Baldwin as Prime Minister was known to have assigned the task of choosing his successor. The most proficient Greek scholar teaching in Oxford at that time was beyond question J. D. Denniston, whose famous book *The Greek Particles* had appeared in 1934. But Murray thought particles a dull subject, and thought that Denniston lacked what he used to call 'originality'. Bowra tells us in his *Memories* that he himself was convinced that Denniston ought to be appointed, but that once he became aware that Murray was unlikely to recommend Denniston, he began to consider himself a candidate. When the choice fell upon E. R. Dodds, at that time Professor of Greek at Birmingham, Bowra was bitterly disappointed, and it cannot be said that he did much to make life easier for the new professor, with whom he was later on friendly terms, but only after many years had passed. But it was not long before Bowra became aware that Cyril Bailey's consoling remark that the apparent disaster might prove to be a blessing in disguise had been fully justified.

During the winter of 1936–7 Bowra was absent from Oxford as Visiting Professor at Harvard, where he stayed in Lowell House. He made a powerful impression on both colleagues and audiences, and as usual made good friends. Among the older people, he saw much of John Livingston Lowes, of Felix Frankfurter, and of William James, the son of William and nephew of Henry; amongst the younger, he made friends with Harry Levin, F. O. Matthiessen, and Ted Spencer. Among the classical scholars he had friendly contacts with Carl Jackson and with E. K. Rand; but the most significant of his friendships was with John Finley, who was later to be his colleague as Eastman Professor at Oxford.

Before the end of his visit, Bowra was offered a permanent post at
Harvard, and had to think hard before declining. He was surely
right. Though he was anything but insular, Bowra was too English
to have settled down anywhere outside England, perhaps too
Oxonian to have settled down outside Oxford.

In 1938 the Warden of Wadham retired from office, and though
only forty years of age Bowra was put forward for the succession
by Wade-Gery together with Professor F. A. Lindemann, later
Lord Cherwell. Considering the difference in their political
opinions, it may seem strange to find Lindemann as one of Bowra's
strongest advocates; but over the then all-important question of
Chamberlain's policy of appeasing Hitler they were in close agreement.

Not surprisingly, the news of Bowra's election came as a shock
to that section of opinion which he would have described as *bien-
pensant*. He was, as the *Times* obituary notice of him says, 'a free
thinker, an epicure and an uninhibited advocate of pleasure';
worse still, many of his epigrams about respected persons and
institutions had got about. Soon after his election at Wadham,
some of his friends outside that college entertained him at a party
held to celebrate his triumph; they ended by celebrating black
mass in a college chapel – not his own – and were ejected by the
verger. It was predicted that Bowra would be the greatest possible
failure as the head of a college. In the event, he was generally
acknowledged to have proved the greatest possible success.

Fortunately for Wadham College, though less fortunately for
the common good, Bowra was never offered a government post
during the war. If he had been, the result might have been
remarkable. The powers that enabled Bowra to master the contents
of innumerable books in a short time served him well in gaining
a rapid grasp of business. His gift for understanding the working
of other people's minds helped him to find the arguments that
would convince them, and he was able to get through the agenda
quickly without giving his colleagues the feeling that they had
been hurried into acquiescence. His remarkable gift for discerning
ability in others led to some wise choices in fellowship elections,
and he maintained the friendliest relations with his colleagues,
guiding and encouraging the younger ones without ever seeming
to patronise them. Every undergraduate in the college got a vivid
impression of the Warden's personality, and knew that he placed

nothing before the education and welfare of the junior members of the university.

Bowra's *Sophoclean Tragedy* appeared in 1944; it had been written a good deal earlier, but its publication was delayed because of the war. Its distinguishing note is the contention that in Sophocles' work the justice of the gods is upheld. Although some psychological arguments that do not convince are used, and at times the nature of divine justice seems to be conceived in too uncomplicated a fashion, the book is a valuable contribution to the understanding of the poet.

As early as 1934, Bowra had written for his own amusement a study of Yeats. He had become friends with Yeats, who for some time lived in Oxford; he showed Yeats an early draft, and Yeats's comments on it are to be found in *Memories* (p. 240). Other essays about modern poets followed, and these finally appeared in the volume *The Heritage of Symbolism* (1943); besides Yeats, there are chapters on Valéry, Rilke, George, and Blok. This publication and that of *From Virgil to Milton* (1945), a valuable study of the secondary epic, made possible Bowra's election to the Oxford Chair of Poetry, a post held for five-year periods, which he occupied from 1946 to 1951; the renewed interest in this chair and its occupants dates from the period of his tenure. By way of an inaugural lecture, he gave under the title of 'The Background of Modern Poetry' a lucid and intelligent account of the aims and presuppositions of the modern movement. In 1949 he published *The Creative Experiment*, a kind of sequel to *The Heritage of Symbolism*, in which he discussed Cavafy, Apollinaire, Mayakovsky, Pasternak's early poetry, Eliot's *The Waste Land*, Lorca's *Romancero Gitano*, and Rafael Alberti's *Sobre los Angeles*. *The Romantic Imagination* (1950) contains lectures given when he was Charles Eliot Norton Professor at Harvard in 1948–9, staying at Eliot House under the auspices of his old friend John Finley. Many of the essays on modern and medieval poetry which he composed subsequently are reprinted in the volume *In General and Particular* (1964). Special mention may be made of 'The Simplicity of Racine', where his familiarity with certain of the poet's sources gave him an advantage over other Racinian critics, and of his Taylorian Lecture of 1961 on 'Poetry and the First World War', a subject on which he was particularly well qualified to speak. In 1965 he gave the Wiles Lectures at the Queen's University,

Belfast, which appeared the following year under the title *Poetry and Politics, 1900–1960;* the book contains interesting remarks about poets whom he knew, like Edith Sitwell, Quasimodo, Seferis, and Neruda.

'If we do not know what an author has tried to do,' Bowra once wrote, 'we cannot justly decide whether he has succeeded in doing it.' Much of his critical work was designed to answer just this question. He concentrates on an attempt to explain the author's artistic purpose and the method he has used in order to achieve it; he would have agreed with Carlyle that to read any author properly one must as far as possible enter into his mind and see with his eyes. The catholicity of his taste and the warmth of his enthusiasm for literature enabled Bowra to do this effectively in the case of many different writers; and at a time when some of the most influential literary critics were restricted in their interests and narrow in their sympathies, these qualities made his writings especially valuable. The merits of his critical writings are balanced by marked deficiencies. That very enthusiasm for authors which was one of his chief assets was a disadvantage insofar as it caused his approach to authors to be descriptive rather than critical. Too often his descriptions have a kind of cosiness, as though all were for the best in the best of possible worlds; and this effect is strengthened by the flatness of much of the writing. It is instructive to compare his work with that of another critic of comparably wide sympathies, Edmund Wilson. One cannot imagine a scholar like Bowra being as misguided as Wilson was over the *Philoctetes* of Sophocles or the Dead Sea Scrolls; yet by comparison Bowra's critical writings lack a cutting edge. Bowra is most successful with those modern poets who stand closest to the romantic tradition, particularly his friend Yeats; he is less at home with Eliot, as his careful but uninspired summary of *The Waste Land* shows. But even this essay is a far more valuable guide to someone not yet acquainted with the poet or his methods than many more penetrating critical studies would supply; and this is true of most of Bowra's criticism.

Bowra should by right have succeeded to the Vice-Chancellorship of Oxford in 1948, when an unforeseen accident removed the then incumbent; but he was then at Harvard, and so was enabled to serve out his term as Professor of Poetry and then be Vice-Chancellor from 1951 to 1954. His tenure of the post was the most memorable of modern times. The qualities that made him such

a successful head of his own college stood him in good stead
in this office also. He was an effective chairman of committees,
able to master great masses of material with impressive speed
and altogether free from the inability to decide which is such
an infuriating characteristic of academic persons. His swiftness
in repartee silenced antagonists; and his brilliant conversation,
combined with a good nature remarkable in one so witty and
always more in evidence as he grew older, made him countless
friends. After he had ceased to be Vice-Chancellor Bowra was re-
elected to the Hebdomadal Council by a number of votes far in
excess of any previously recorded, and continued to serve on this
body, on the General Board, the University Chest, and as a Delegate of the Clarendon Press, and did valuable service to all these
bodies. He was much concerned to see that important posts, and
also honorary degrees, should go to the best candidates, and his
great power to recognise ability in others helped him to do the
university specially valuable service in this respect. The promin-
ence on university committees of a person of so much scholarly
distinction and of such a cosmopolitan outlook did much to redeem
Oxford from the reproach of parochialism, which in earlier times
might justly have been levelled at it.

The British Academy also profited from Bowra's great admini-
strative ability. He had become a Fellow in 1938 and was President
from 1958 to 1962. In two matters in particular, that of the
Treasury Grant and of the setting up of a British Institute in
Teheran, he did the Academy great service;[1] but his work for the
Academy will be chronicled elsewhere (see p. 130).

This public activity never diminished the flow of Bowra's
writings, and his best written work, with the exception of his early
book about the *Iliad*, belongs to the last part of his career. The
later works dealing with modern poetry have already been described.
Heroic Poetry (1952) shows an astonishing knowledge of primary
epic literature in many languages, and presents its results in most
attractive fashion; hardly any other scholar could have written
this book. The same is true of *Primitive Song* (1962), which offers
translations from the verse of those communities which may be
thought to give a notion of the primitive way of life. Bowra's
large contribution to the study of epic poetry was rounded off by

---

[1] See Sir Mortimer Wheeler's *The British Academy, 1949–68*.

C

a posthumously published book entitled *Homer*, written for the series 'Classical Life and Letters', and giving a clear and extremely up-to-date account of the Homeric poems. Here Bowra works out ideas already touched on in his Andrew Lang Lecture of 1955, 'Homer and his Forerunners'. While fully taking into account the work of Milman Parry, Bowra showed how its acceptance was perfectly consistent with a unitarianism, placing Homer at the end of a long poetic tradition, of the kind advocated in *Tradition and Design in the Iliad* forty-two years earlier.

Bowra meant his *Pindar* (1964) to be his main achievement in scholarship. Not everyone will think it was. Two years before its publication, Elroy L. Bundy had challenged the assumption that Pindar's odes of victory were full of personal and historical allusions, and had insisted that the main clue to their interpretation lay in the truth that the poet's primary purpose was to praise the victor he was celebrating (see now *Journal of Hellenic Studies* 93, 1973, 109 ff.). Bowra's book never questions the assumption of Wilamowitz that a study of Pindar can take the form of a biography. Unlike Wilamowitz, he did not give his book a biographical form, but to reject the analysis of individual poems in favour of chapters each devoted to some general topic was a still greater error. The mass of generalisation becomes tedious, and the style tends more than usually towards cliché. The *Pindar* is indeed a useful book. Bowra was familiar with the whole relevant literature; he took far more trouble over detail than he had in *Greek Lyric Poetry* in 1936; and his obvious affection for his subject lends the work a special attraction. But it breaks no new ground, and can hardly be compared with Bowra's work on Homer.

Some of Bowra's early articles were collected in the volume *Problems in Greek Poetry* (1954); articles of the later period are reprinted in *In Greek Margins* (1970). These articles, particularly the later ones, contain some of Bowra's best classical work. He would take an individual work, usually a poem, often one that had suffered neglect because of its isolation, and would explain its significance and relate it to historical context.

Bowra was the successor of his teacher, Gilbert Murray, as the leading provider of works designed to explain Greek literature to the English-speaking general reader; and the *Times* obituary well says that if Murray's style was the more delicate instrument, Bowra was more direct and realistic. As early as 1935 he contributed to the Home University Library a small but useful book called *Ancient Greek Literature*. In 1957 he brought out *The Greek Experience*, a well-written and carefully considered book which is generally considered the best work of its kind now available in English. *Landmarks in Greek Literature* (1966) is another valuable survey; and *Periclean Athens* (1971) is not only full of information but reveals a gift for historical narrative that makes the reader wish Bowra had essayed it earlier.

Bowra would normally have vacated the Wardenship of Wadham in 1968, when he reached the age of seventy. But the Fellows honoured him by using their power to extend his tenure for two years; and when in 1970 that period expired, they granted him the unusual privilege of continuing to occupy rooms in college. Here he died suddenly, as he would have wished, on 4 July 1971. In spite of increasing deafness, he had retained all his powers to the last.

Bowra's achievement as a scholar and critic is, by any standards, considerable; his career as a university administrator is the most distinguished of modern England. Yet his most remarkable success lies in his influence on those who encountered him in Oxford. This influence was powerful throughout his career, but most of all in the early part of it; later it was more widely diffused but less highly concentrated.

An important element in his influence was the brilliance of his talk. But Bowra was far more than an amusing talker; he was, in Sir Isaiah Berlin's words, 'a major liberating influence'. In Bowra's early years in Oxford the constricting stuffiness of Victorian convention still lay heavily on much of English social life. Much of intellectual life was correspondingly inhibited; till well into the thirties most senior academics and schoolmasters reacted with sheer horror to any movement in literature and the arts that seemed to break away from the Victorian tradition. Against this tradition Bowra was an open rebel. He was ready, and had been since his early years, to lend an ear to innovations in art and literature. He had a kind of religion, like that of the early Greeks, but he did not believe in Christianity, and would have agreed with Keynes in finding it odd of so many earnest Victorian atheists to go on proving it to be false and wishing it were true. He enjoyed pleasure, and thought that on the whole what people liked tended to be good for them.

In politics, his sympathies, like those of many generous-minded members of his generation, were with the left rather than the right; but not all modern left-wingers could safely claim him as a kindred spirit. During the General Strike of 1926 his sympathies were with the strikers; he was a close friend of Hugh Gaitskell; and after the Papadopoulos government came to power in Greece, he gave up the Hellenic Cruises that had been one of his favourite recreations. During the thirties he campaigned actively against the policy of appeasing National Socialist Germany. Dislike of appeasement was by no means confined to left-wingers; but Bowra loathed everything that was associated with the predominance of men like Baldwin and Neville Chamberlain. Yet he was never a doctrinaire socialist; anyone in doubt on the matter should study the references in his *Memories* to the late Lord Lindsay of Birker, Master of Balliol. His left-wing sympathies arose from his desire for liberty, which in his youth was threatened chiefly by right-wing and conventionally religious authoritarians. He did not care for cant; and in his later years, when most cant was coming from the left, he did not allow ideological sympathies to blind him to its nature. One of his strongest terms of disapproval was 'cagey'; he detested the stuffy, cautious conventionality that is epitomised by his friend Anthony Powell's famous character, Kenneth Widmerpool. Bowra did what he could to block the advance of Oxford's Widmerpools, of whatever political colouring.

Unlike most people who talk a great deal, Bowra was uncannily observant of others and alive to their reactions. No one was more generous in giving encouragement to others, and in England, where reserve and the cult of good form so often damp enthusiasm, this quality was particularly precious. The number of people who acknowledge a debt to Bowra for having strengthened their self-confidence at a critical period is very great; the people in question are of very different kinds, and many exceptionally gifted. When Bowra had reached a position in which he could use his gift of discerning talent by promoting able people, he spared no pains to do so. During his last months he was in hospital suffering from a painful complaint when he was informed that a gifted young scholar, whose promise he had long before discerned, had been appointed to a high position. Bowra was so excited that he almost leaped out of bed in his delight.

Those who knew only Bowra's writings may find it hard to

understand, but no person who knew him at all well can fail to be surprised, that nothing that he ever wrote gives the faintest inkling of the impression which he made in conversation. He wrote indeed better than most scholars, and especially in the later part of his career he knew how to order his material with great skill. But even where he avoids cliché, what he wrote seems flat and pedestrian beside the brilliance of what he said. To this deficiency of style corresponds a deficiency of content. His work in technical scholarship is solid, sound, judicious, but it is never brilliant; his criticism is sane, lucid, sympathetic, but it lacks flair.

How can we explain this puzzling limitation? We have seen that he himself wrote of his lack of self-confidence in early life; and something of this uncertainty always remained with him. One sign of it was his extreme sensitivity to adverse criticism; at a hint of disloyalty he could become furious even with old friends. Sir Isaiah Berlin thinks that his self-confidence was undermined by the destructive criticism of H. W. B. Joseph, but the roots of his diffidence must lie further back. At school he had disliked the hard grammatical grind of the old-fashioned classical education; he came to love the ancient authors during the war, when he read them for pleasure, just as he read Anatole France, Verlaine, or Baudelaire. He read rapidly, and his quickly-moving brain tended to bypass difficulties; he seldom stopped to break his head over a knotty problem. At Oxford he became well aware of his deficiencies; he was aware of the difference between his scholarship and that of men like Housman or Lobel, and though he knew that he was capable of some achievements which they never attempted, the knowledge worried him. But by an act of will he gave himself the resolution necessary to carry through each plan; he tapped speedily away on his typewriter, seldom pausing for reflection, for too much reflection might weaken his determination. As in technical scholarship he made mistakes until he learned not to expose his weakest side, so in criticism he failed to come to grips with the chief critical problems; that very sympathy with the authors whom he studied that was one of his best qualities had also its reverse side. Cyril Connolly has said that he was a poet *manqué*.[1] Certainly his talk was more like a creative writer's than like a scholar's, and if he had essayed creative writing perhaps he would have shed some of his inhibitions. Scholarship gave him a discipline he needed; and yet

[1] See p. 45.

it may have promoted what Sir Isaiah calls 'a peculiar lack of faith in his original and splendid gifts'. His least inhibited writing was his occasional verse, and it is sad that little of this is likely to be published while those who can recognise its allusions are alive.

But his achievements are so considerable that the regret felt by his friends that he did not accomplish more is a striking tribute to the power of his personality. He was the most celebrated Oxford character since Jowett, whom he surpassed in scholarship and in warmth of character. His services to his college and his university were unique; so was his effect upon colleagues and undergraduates of all kinds, obscure as well as famous. But when all this has been said, it gives no notion of what it was like to talk with him, and still less of the affection and admiration felt for him, at least during his later years, by all who knew him.

4

Mercurius Oxoniensis

Glorious Reign of Sir Maurice, decd.

Good brother Londiniensis,

I am now released from canon Goosegrass's fruit-cage and hasten to send you, as I have promised, a brief accompt of our great wit, Sir Maurice Bowra, lately deceas'd; though I hope that a better pen than mine will eternize his virtues in your friend's new *Athenae Oxonienses*. But haply my rude rubble will furnish mortar for other men's building, and so, without more ado, I shall begin.

He was of a family long rooted in Kent, but branching out (for severall descents) into China; in which far country he was born, *anno* 1898, and retain'd an affection for it through all its late mutations. He was school'd in England, at Cheltenham, a very regular place. *Anno* 1917 he went to the warre in Flanders, and was in some bloody actions there, which gave him a lasting distaste to that whole business, so that he would never thereafter endure martiall talk. *Dulce bellum inexpertis;* but he had try'd it. After our victory he went up to New-coll. in Oxon, where his sprightly wit, in those merry times, at once made him famous among his co-temporaries and his learning in the antient tongues commended him to his seniors, so that, *anno* 1922, he became Fellow of Wadham coll.; and surely that poor college never made a happier election.

He was a conviviall soul, preferring above all others the best Rhenish wines (as indeed they are delicious), which he would buy only from Jews in Frankfort; for he loved not your true nordick Germans. His entertainment in those days was famous. He was a friend of the young and mightily encouraged the true wits amongst 'em, who never forgot that encouragement. 'Tis pity our modern dons do so little in that sort: 'tis of more value than all their niggling research. His wit was loud and pungent, deliver'd at large in publick places, with a great boom which could be heard,

* Published in *The Spectator* on 9 October 1971

reverberating, in the next quadrangle; but being so free and open, 'twas innocent, like a humble-bee on a heath, which, though it hit you on the nose, rather startles than stings. And yet he could be fierce too, if cross'd, and would roar like a lyon. I have heard of two Fellows of Wadham coll. blown clean out of different windows with a single snort. But these tempests were soon over and the sun thereafter (if duly propitiated with litanies and sacrifice) would come forth again, fresh and warm.

He was an excellent Grecian and at one time (*anno* 1936) aspired to the Regius Chair in that hall of learning, but was disappointed. He took such disappointments ill, and would spend the shafts of his wit upon his conquerours to show that there at least he was invincible. But he dipp'd not those shafts in malice : wit was his only revenge. Nor did he suffer long under this discomfiture. For two years later he was elected Warden of his coll., and celebrated his victory by a merry symposiack with some young wits in Merton coll.; after which (the wine being choice and copious), he was inspired to enter the chapel and deliver a sermon, *extempore*, from the pulpit, till driven thence by the verger. Though his homily was thus unprepared, I doubt not that 'twas both witty and resonant, though whether sound in doctrine is a question. He is thought to be the only Head of a college to be church-outed by a verger for brawling.

After this unusuall inauguration, he ruled his coll. with great prudence for 32 years and rais'd it up mightily, both in learning, by his wise choice of Fellows, and in wealth, by doubling its numbers. 'Tis said that after the late warre, when men pressed from all quarters into Oxon, he had seven Americans in every bed, all paying full fees; whereby that coll., from poor, became rich; which is a better way of draining that Euphrates than by going over there, as some of our Heads do, and rattling the poor-box from coast to coast, and city to city.

He went thither himself, *anno* 1948, but for honest purposes, *viz:* to lecture on Poësy at Harvard coll. 'Twas an ill-judg'd time, as it fell out; for first, when he arrived there, he found that whole society flocking to the lectures of our incomparable wit, Sir Esay Berlin, with whom 'tis vain to contend; and then, while he was there, behold! a tragedy in Oxon : for our worthy Vice-chancellour, Dr Stallybrass, the great lawyer, fell out of a train (he was returning from a law-feast in London), to the great loss both of the

university and of Brazen-nose coll., of which he was Principal; to
whom, by the *rota* then in force (*anglicè* Buggins' turn), our Sir
Maurice should have succeeded; but being absent, he lost it to the
Dean of Christchurch, Dr Lowe, who was waiting next in the
queue; which miffed him. Also, he liked not their way of life in
those parts, and least of all their dinners, as too insipid for his
taste; to relieve which he had food-parcels sent out to him from
England, thus reversing the usual course; for 'twas generally
thought, at that time, that we here were all starving and only kept
alive by hampers of clam, spam, doughnuts, peanuts, etc., sent over
from those Plantations.

He succeeded as Vice-chancellour at the next turn, *anno* 1951,
and 'twas a glorious reign. His predecessor Dr Lowe (a Scotchman out of Canada) had been thought somewhat frugall in his
entertainment; but in the twinkling of an eye that was all changed.
He was a brisk man of business too, doving expedition, not for-
mality, and would roughly abbreviate the rituall dances of the
Wykehamicall brethren. When he graduated the boys, he would
swat 'em sharply on the head, like studs on a conveyor-belt, with
cap or Bible indifferently (for he did not distinguish much between
the instruments). He suffer'd not committees to keep him from
more agreeable colloquies. 'Tis said he once despatch'd all the
business of the Generall Board (a taedious body) in ten minutes.

He was a rare judge of men, so that his voice, in all our elections,
had great power. He valued men by their wits, not their morales,
and cared not if the graver sort were outraged. He procured
doctorates, *honoris causâ*, for some questionable *virtuosi*: one of
our Vice-chancellours (a severe Scotchman) refused to admit one
such to his table, as having incorrect tastes in love, although 'twas
but luncheon, and the risque was slight. 'Twas Monsieur Gide, I
think; who, feasting instead with Sir Maurice and Mistress
Starkie, enjoyed perhaps a more joviall collation. He was not afraid
to measure his own deserts either. Once, as Vice-chancellour, he
nominated himself to a lifelong post of honour and profit, ingenu-
ously declaring that he knew none fitter for such a place; which
silenced all debate. I doubt not that he was right.

In academick statecraft he aimed at victory, and generally won
it; for he knew his own mind, and when to change it, which he
could do very swiftly, none noticing, not even himself. So he prevail'd over the generality of our senatours, who either think not

at all, or know not what they think, or, having come painfully to their thoughts, persevere too stiffly in them. If he was ever defeated (as must happen to all), he had a sovereign balm against that hurt: for he quickly convinced himself that he had always been on the contrary side; nay, had himself led it to victory.

In Wadham coll. he ruled absolutely. The late Lord Cherwell (who had very different principles) was a Fellow of that coll., but those two great states-men were wary beasts who knew each other's strength and chose to keep the peace; which was as well, for when they clash'd, head on, the forest trembled. Besides, the Warden was at home only in Oxon, where he knew every secret spring and college trough, whereas his Lordship had another water-hole, at the back door of Downing-street in London, which he preferr'd.

Though thus busy with academick power, he did not for that forsake his studies (as too many of our senatours do), but found time for 'em in the midst of his avocations, and plied 'em busily. His prime care was for Greek letters, but he knew many modern tongues too, which all, in his mouth, sounded the same. He was an unfeigned lover of the Muses (or some of them: not musick or paintery), and writ much upon poësy, whether antient or modern, heroick, lyrick, or symbolicall. His writing was rather copious and fluent than originall or durable, for he writ as he spake, freely, staying not to correct or polish. But there is wit in it, and philosophy too. His *Greek Experience* is an excellent book (heed not the grammarians): 'tis his *credo*. He edited Pindar in octavo. His last book, newly printed, I await from the bookseller. In his younger days he also writ sharp satires, in verse, on his friends (and sharper still on his enemies), which, happily, few have seen. 'Tis said the manuscript lies safely hid in the *escritoire* of a lady of title and fashion. But later, in his *Memoires*, he made peace with all men.

He travelled much, especially to Greece, and of late years was much priz'd as a lecturer on cruises among those delicate isles. He liked that style of discourse, as more free and better suited to his genius than academick lectures. He was much courted by the itinerant ladies, though some of 'em complain'd that he eluded 'em at dinner, preferring certain ingeniose peeresses, who (being old friends) easily entrapp'd him and kept him to themselves. His great rival on those cruises was Sir Mortimer Wheeler, that venerable master of Antiquity. 'Twas a mistake for those two eminent men to go on the same boat. They only did it once. 'Tis said that Sir Mortimer prevail'd in the contest, and that Sir Maurice, like Achilles, retreated to his cabin, where he stayed, inexorable, till the ship was dock'd. But the ladies of quality saw to it that he starved not, feeding him privily on broiled sword-fish and Samian wine.

He continued these voyages till the present martiall tyrants usurp'd power in Greece, after which he could never be prevail'd upon to go thither. For he was always a great defender of liberty, sweet liberty, at least upon its right-hand side (on the other, he was less vigilant), and would readily give his name, without much enquiry, to any cause whose advocates were prudent enough to use that blessed word; in which he was not alone in his time.

When he ceas'd to rule over his college, he lived on there in a pretty set of rooms in the new quadrangle (to be call'd by his name), where he receiv'd his friends and exercised that praerogative of age which is to make nice observations upon younger men. His worthy successour, Master Hampshire (an old friend), treated him with great civility. He died as he would have wished, suddenly: the lamp blew out after a day spent convivially with his old pupills. Truly, we shall long lament his loss, for as, by his wit and conversation, he enhanced the life of our society, so he look'd not, in other men, for learning only (though a great respecter of that), but also for that vitall force which animates and unites true learning, else dead and useless. In short, he knew the purpose of a university better than those who have writ most about it: which is, to draw the young towards sound learning, and good letters, and the taste of life. The rest are foibles; at least in the eyes of

Your loving friend

Mercurius Oxoniensis

5

Cyril Connolly

Hedonist and Stoic

A few weeks ago Maurice Bowra was alive: his massive head replete with value judgments, innumerable lines of poetry in many languages, a complete card index of stories about his friends, seventy-four years of discrimination, affection, love, memories of old battles, all rendered in his unforgettable voice with its fastidious rasping musical glow, an epigram whistling over like an untakeable service, a qualification or a pun woven into the verdict. Meanwhile the eyes cast a cold look; blue eyes wide apart in a low forehead over which his brown hair used to fall, *gli occhi onesti e tardi*, eyes of a platoon commander in the First World War which had seen death and estimated the casualties. A trace of sensuality about the mouth, the lips rather full but a face in which everything was under control. 'Whatever you hear about the war,' he told me, 'remember it was far far worse: inconceivably bloody – nobody who wasn't there can ever imagine what it was like.' He was one of the Marathonomachoi, young men whose initiation into life was shell-fire, mud and gangrene, the mowing down of their friends by machine guns.

These experiences were only four or five years behind him when we first met. He was then a young don at Wadham who, with Urquhart, Harrod and Dundas, were among those who encouraged a few undergraduates at a time, piloting them through the shoals of adolescence, the clashing rocks of penury and passion.

> When days are long and sunny
> The flower of youth is blown
> We waste our parents' money
> And time that is our own.

As I wrote in imitation of Housman, for to me Oxford was no

* Published in the *Sunday Times Magazine* on 29 August 1971 and reprinted in *The Evening Colonnade*, 23 June 1972

celestial city but a place where I was unhappier than I had ever been before. I could have got a good first in nervous breakdowns. It was then I came to know Maurice well; he saved me from despair; his method was to draw one out about parents and friends, making a kind of therapeutic pack of cards which were then dealt out as one makes a sad child laugh – 'What does Major Connolly think of the *Après-midi d'un Faune?*' He would introduce me to some of his older friends like Philip Ritchie with a genial, 'This is Connolly. Coming man. (Pause.) Hasn't come yet' – and he introduced me also to modern literature, to the Renaissance that was in flower all about us, Eliot, Proust, the later Yeats, Hardy's poetry, Edith Sitwell – and to many byways of Greek and Latin. This was an overwhelming experience because in both our cases the seed fell on good ground. The books we loved grew and sprouted in the mind. I read in *The Times* that there were many who thought Maurice was wasted at Oxford, that his administrative talents and energy would have found better expression in politics; this may have been the case but I am convinced that his tragedy, since every man has a tragedy, is that he was not a poet. Such a lifetime's devotion to the critique of poetry must have been the sign of a poet manqué. From the cauldron of his heart emerged only a few bubbles – intricate metallic satires on some of his friends, metrical *tours de force* like the derision of Donne or Archilochus, the only kind of poetry nobody could make fun of.

Maurice had the verbal gifts, the energy, the high romantic imagination to be a great poet, fit companion to Yeats and Hardy, but there was an intractable inhibition, a block resulting from some parental situation or possibly the trauma of the trenches. He needed very strong doses of both work and pleasure; his appreciation of poetry formed the bulk of his work but, like a poet, he rode high above the academic honours which were showered on him; nobody who formed part of his circle was ever made aware of all his degrees and doctorates, of his endless unfussy toil as vice-chancellor or as head of a college. He never spoke of a pupil except to put the best face on his problems or to suggest how he could help him. Behind the hedonist rode the stoic emperor, even as the platoon commander incorporated into himself the heroes of the *Iliad* or the athletes of Pindar.

The superb tribute in *The Times* mentioned a particular aspect of his middle period, the 'periods of estrangement in his younger days even from his best friends'. I have known what it is to be hated by Maurice and I spent several years in the wilderness; it was a devastating experience. One would wake up in the middle of the night and seem to hear that inexorable luncheon-party voice roar over one like a bulldozer.

What is so remarkable is that this menacing Olympian demigod who used all his advantages to lay about him among the mortals who crossed his path should have mellowed into such a rock-like friend and counsellor.

To understand him as a person one must know that he was deeply romantic. When I first met him he told me about the tigers swimming over to Formosa from the mainland, which set them above all other tigers, and his first group of friends were also mysteriously superior. He saw human life as a tragedy in which great poets were the heroes who fought back and tried to give life a meaning. Such rebels formed the background of his early admirations, or handsome ill-fated dandies like Philip Ritchie and Adrian Bishop.

His romanticism came out in his choice of women friends. He loved several women profoundly and spoke of them in terms of deep devotion; they were all strong characters, 'doctae puellae', in the world but not worldly; and they too were generous and brave and loyal, qualities which he admired almost more than brains and beauty. He had thought of marrying, but I think his genius demanded an inner privacy which would never have tolerated the wear and tear of proximity. 'I am the last male Bowra,' he wrote to me. He loved children and his last day on earth was packed with two weddings and a dinner party for young colleagues.

Genius? Yes – in the sense in which Dr Johnson was a genius, in being a person sculpted out of a harder, grander material than anybody else. His talk, with its play on words as a means to identification of improbable affinities, its bizarre surrealism, its teasing understatement, will never be correctly remembered, his books are largely collections of lectures and his style is somewhat lifeless, his autobiography too well-mannered, though if we know how to look for it, the truth is there. His satires remain unprintable even privately,[1] so we return to the personality itself, the enthusiast, the friend, the liberator, the protector, hero and humanist, wit and scholar, the granite substance and inflexible toughness beneath

[1] But see pp. 76 ff. (Ed.).

the epicurean respect for pleasure. Yet his researches into the
origins of poetry, the passage from incantation to song, from song
to epic, from epic to the written word, aided by his knowledge of
languages and his passion for the Mediterranean are truly creative,
his book on the Greek experience a masterpiece of concision, his
Penguin Pindar of translation. *The Heritage of Symbolism* and
The Creative Experiment are among the best commentaries on the
moderns. Yeats wrote a poem to him and Pasternak a wonderful
letter. He wrote good letters, too: 'I was a little perplexed when
you challenged me with making Hardy my god and not Eliot. In
fact my god from 1917 onwards was Yeats, and then Hardy –
Hardy, because he alone expressed my cosmic despair as a young
man, when I was flung into the war, which was plainly mad and
unspeakably horrible. I never talk of it, and put it out of my
mind, but Hardy did a lot to heal my wounds, and that is why I
forgive him his many inept and absurd lines and comical choice
of words. He is *not* of the breed of Mallarmé, but he is in his
own way a sort of saint, and that touched me more than Eliot did
at the start. Eliot hit me very hard inside, but I resisted it, because
I could not quite believe that everything was so drab as he said,
and I resisted the Christian part. But now I see that he was on
the whole right, and that the Christian part is in fact hardly
Christian at all, but really a plea for the inner life.'

I saw him just before he died in the new flat Wadham had made
over to him. He talked about his 'breathing-troubles' as 'just one
of the things one has to expect from old age' – and I said I put
blindness, being totally bedridden and dropping dead as the worst,
in that order. 'Dropping dead,' he boomed, 'has no terrors for me.'

He has meant so much to so many people for so long that his
friends are still suffering from delayed shock, the oracle silenced,
the bastion fallen.

$$\text{ἀπέσβετο καὶ λάλον ὕδωρ}^1$$

---

[1] 'The talking well's run dry'. See his essay 'The Last Oracle' in *On Greek
Margins*, p. 233.

6

Noel Annan

A Man I Loved

I was going to pick up Maurice for Sunday lunch when they telephoned and said he was dead. Later that week I was standing on a
sunny, sultry Oxford afternoon gazing down at his coffin, in which
the hideous processes of corruption were already at work: the
darkness which was about to close over it was the symbol of all
that he detested most. So ended the days of a man I loved, a creator
who made his friends part of what they are.

The dead can speak only through their own writings, and, as is
often said, Bowra's published works give no inkling of what his
conversation was like. Even his letters are not to be trusted: they
mislead the reader because so often they express the dead man's
exasperation that life is not fairer or men wiser. But in them, his
tone of voice can at any rate be heard.[1] That voice . . . Echoes of
its intonations and inflections reverberated through Oxford and
London. People who had never met him used his phrases; Evelyn
Waugh's undergraduate diaries are full of them, though at that
time he was not one of Maurice's friends; and at least one of his
friends acquired his voice and manner lock, stock and barrel, as if
it had been auctioned. His voice had the carrying power of the
Last Trump, but when he lowered it and spoke as if imparting a
confidence the affection within his nature rose to the surface until,
as if alarmed that there was something the matter with him, he
reasserted himself as the archangel and blew a tremendous blast.
Using the notation of *Hymns Ancient and Modern* you could score
an utterance as follows: 'They are a particularly agreeable pair.
(*dim*) I enjoyed my visit with them (*pp.*) enormously. (*ff.*)
ENORMOUSLY.' The roar so beat about your ears that you
found yourself roaring too as the weekend drew to a close.

It was at weekends that I got to know him – at weekends on

---

[1] In quoting from these letters below I have at times had to use pseudo-
nyms and to make minor emendations.

leave during the war with Dadie Rylands at King's who gave me this as so many good things. To meet him was like downing tumblers of brandy rather than savouring a bottle of wine. One left reeling. No one remotely resembled him at Cambridge. At King's we had our sprightly moments, but when we discussed grave dilemmas of the heart or mind, we flowed like streams, sometimes in flood, sometimes meandering; we were even known to dry up and fall into bottomless silences if we caught ourselves saying something which was technically nonsense or which might not be true. Truth and friendship – these were our simple ideals, though we knew them to be derided by such characteristic Oxonians as Philip Toynbee. Maurice's conversation was not remotely comparable. Like the *Royal Sovereign* breaking the line at Trafalgar, all cannon double-shotted, he fired deafening broadsides. Spars ignited, mizzen top-masts crashed to the decks, studding sails were blown overboard, splinters ricocheted inflicting fearful wounds on friend and foe alike. But when the smoke cleared you found that you had all the time been sitting in the stalls witnessing a splendid transformation scene in a pantomime. What he said, or what he wrote in his letters, expressed the world which he invented and was subject to all the complexities of appearance and reality, *Sein und Schein*, that he knew so well in literature; he never suffered from the delusion that the world which his wit created was a may of actuality. You realised that you yourself, like everyone else, including those most devoted, would be impaled upon his scandalous, reckless comments. It did not matter: they were his contribution to what he called the Higher Truth, not to be confined by the shackles of scholarly accuracy from which in the life which he shared with his friends he was glad to be relieved. This much you took for granted.

From Maurice you also took for granted warmth, generosity, devotion, loyalty. When he writes, 'It has been a bloody time. Humphrey's death robs me of my most distinguished and most interesting colleague. Tom Dunbabin, a heroic archaeologist, is dying of cancer which the doctors diagnosed for seven weeks as lumbago,' the words do not begin to express his grief and hatred of death. You could not forget how he would catch your arm in a grip which stopped the circulation, or the way he would hug one of his favourite girls, lifting them off the ground if they were his size or standing on tiptoe if they towered above him; but how can

D

you convey his emotion? Some who possess all the virtues lower
the temperature when they enter a room. When Maurice entered,
it shot up. He warmed his friends; and he lived most intensely
when they were about him. He did not care much for the *beau
monde* who are always on the search for new acquaintances whom
they then call friends. He belonged to a generation who put
enormous weight on friendship. It was something far more than
casual geniality, it made demands, it imposed duties and much
should be sacrificed for it. It was not to be confused with party
going, still less with *Mitdabeisein*. Friendship implied unreserved
affection and support, but it was a dry fierce heat, not humid;
he was vehement, and he rebuked.

To me he was generous beyond all bounds. When we were just
married and not only had no money but had spent all our rationed
foreign currency, he insisted that we meet him in Rome: from
there he drove us to Naples and on to Amalfi where we stayed
bathing for a week at his expense. 'No stint' was a command-
ment he found easy to obey though, as he sometimes observed,
others seemed ignorant of it. His own hospitality was gargantuan,
his pleasure in food and drink uninhibited, his digestion and
head ironclad. He was as good a guest as host and rewarded those
who entertained him when on holiday abroad with letters of gossip
such as this to Nigel Clive:

'What with picking oakum, working the treadmill and the other
duties of post-war life in Oxford, I have been grossly slow in
writing to thank you for your wonderful kindnesses and
courtesies to me in Athens. The best days were those Sundays –
I shall never forget them with the ghost of Brother Tom brood-
ing benevolently under the yellow umbrella and the various gods
doing their little tricks on us . . . The Honorable Mrs Durdles
is away in Florence. I find it very odd. Antony does not know
when she will come back. "It's a great problem," he says on the
telephone. Can she have an Italian lover? I doubt it with those
pink legs and all that scurf. Professor Dawkins much enjoyed
his operation for prostate and gave interesting details of it.
Betch is much pleased by the extent of his renown in Greece and
has reduced his weekly work to an hour a week and complains
bitterly about it. His wife goes round like a maelstrom and
suckles the children while milking the cow. She is becoming a

perfect Mother India with a touch of Wendy and a look of
Pocahontas . . . Gerald has been made a governor of the
Institute and sends me letters about his support if I do what he
wants to do. I regard this as none too friendly. Colonel Annan
is said to be settling down, but to what?'

Loyalty was not a virtue which he measured out by drops into a
glass. He was unbridled in his loyalty to his friends, and he
expected them to be loyal too. Intellectuals are often not. They are
disliked by other men because they vacillate and move gingerly
to judgments about people, slide away at the first hint of trouble,
see the merits of the other side so clearly, and then decamp when
their friend is in trouble, or worse, when he is in disgrace. They
ridicule the notion that a man has any *a priori* duty to be loyal to
his family: and if not to his family, why then to an institution or
to colleagues? Intellectuals give their first allegiance to ideas, and
(so they believe) to the truth; and if a friend has made what to
them seems to be an error of judgment or taste, still more to have
betrayed an ideal, they do not hesitate to round on him. To them
personal and family loyalty leads at worst to the mafia and at the
least to that closing of the ranks by which the Establishment wards
off menace and excludes anyone who might upset its value
system. Splendid as dedication to ideas can be, intellectuals sometimes forget that it can lead to that humiliating perversion of
the intellect, the defence of the party line, and to the state of
mind where to ditch one's family and friends becomes vir-
tuous.
   Bowra was fierce in loyalty to his ideals. But he differed from
other intellectuals in being even fiercer in loyalty to his friends. If
a choice had to be made between friends and truth, friends won.
His loyalty to people and to institutions was passionate and uncompromising; and if a friend failed for instance to get a post he concealed the blunt truth in comforting him afterwards and took it
out on his opponents. Such tenderness did not extend to them: he
pursued his enemies relentlessly. When he gave the Oration at
the memorial service for his old friend and tutor, Alick Smith, the
air was so dark with the arrows he despatched, like Apollo spread-
ing the plague among the Grecian host before Troy, that you
half-expected groans to arise from the congregation and the guilty
to totter forth from St Mary's and expire stricken on the steps of

the Radcliffe. Loyalty for him was not a simple matter. If anyone outside the circle made a feint at any of his friends, or at any Fellow or undergraduate of Wadham, good, bad or indifferent, thunderbolts were hurled. Within the circle, however, anything could be said about anybody. He could hector, but so long as no mortal sin had been committed he remained unshakable. Towards the end of his life he disapproved of the view on universities, students, literature and the law which John Sparrow was expressing, and both envied and feared the Warden of All Souls' reckless propensity to say or do anything. But he remained obsessed by Sparrow's personality, was as ever amused when they met; and in his letters to me he would speak of him between denunciations with ironical affection. Three friends of his youth were particularly unassailable. With Bob Boothby and Cyril Connolly he felt entirely happy, and the third, Dadie Rylands, for whom in his undergraduate days long ago he had bought silk shirts in the High, could do no wrong. He had other friends in Cambridge, such as the Davids or Joan and Stanley Bennett (who was Vice-President when Maurice was President of the British Academy). But none was held in such esteem as Dadie, of whose delicate perception into the motives of human beings he stood somewhat in awe and to whose judgments on poetry he deferred. Maurice used to regard him in wonder as one who had fought with beasts at Ephesus; and Dadie was indeed the only person whom I ever saw when Maurice was demolishing someone's character unscrupulously, pull him up sharply like a preservationist halting a bulldozer in the act of levelling a grotesque but lovable old building. But that did not prevent him referring to a begging letter for some good cause of the kind which friends send each other in these terms:

'Dadie has sent me a note demanding money with menaces. I paid up at once and had no acknowledgment. The old boy's inability to write is undermining social life – nearly as bad as our friend Frederick, who has been busy seeing to a drummer boy's first communion.'

He wanted his friends to do well. Like Jowett he expected them to make the most of their gifts. Whatever they produced was not enough: they must push on and do better still. He was a genius at awakening self-confidence and dispelling what he used to call 'a sad state of Minko'.[1] Back at Cambridge after the war at a time when I was indeed settling in, but not perhaps settling down, I received an admonition:

'We are all much worried about you – these goings on – most unsuitable in a young don. Hard work, my boy, that is what we expect from you. A good book – it is much needed – no one is writing and our civilisation is going to pot with books on "Planning for God", etc.'

When my book appeared he was lavish in praise – and exhortation. He felt the same about his most brilliant friends. His admiration for Isaiah Berlin was immense and for that very reason his letters abounded in complaints that Isaiah did not publish more and was frittering his splendid gifts away. He found it hard to accept that Isaiah could not have sat down and allowed the typewriter to take over as it did with him. But when Isaiah got the O.M. (an honour he himself would most dearly have liked) he wrote:

'I am delighted about Isaiah. He is much better than all alternatives . . . and very much deserves it. Though like Our Lord and Socrates he does not publish much, he thinks and says a great deal and has had an enormous influence on our times.'

His letters to me were filled with gratitude to those who cared for him.

'I had a nice Christmas as always with the Clarks. Lady Jane was in hospital having an operation – I can't think for what, but it was quite all right and she was visited hourly by members of her family while the rest of us stayed at home and caroused. Dear K. gets nicer and nicer.'

Or

'The Betjemans' new house is charming – Red Gothic, 1860, with Victorian wallpapers and a very indecent picture by Holman

[1] 'Minko' is the German colloquialism for *Minderwertigkeitskomplex*, or inferiority complex.

Hunt. Had an excellent lunch there and afterwards we sang hymns and Victorian songs. Quite like the good old days before Penelope went to Rome.'

Once given, his friendship was hard to lose. I knew one who lost it when Maurice, rightly or wrongly, judged that he had joined a witch-hunt, and since cruelty to human beings and injustice to individuals were cardinal sins, a terrible anathema followed. Nonspeak was a condition anyone might find himself in with Maurice: in this he was not unique among the iconoclasts of the twenties of which he was a leader. But normally he was indulgent to younger friends because he was intrigued if he found that they held to some notion of value that was new to him provided it was not ideological. The loss of any friend, old or young, was not a sorrow, but a blow between the eyes which made him stagger, only to march on, the blood trickling down his face. When Marcus Dick died, who had left Oxford to be a founding professor at East Anglia, he wrote: 'How will Frank do without Marcus? I miss the old boy very much. He really was somebody and had almost no donnish faults.' I remembered Maurice describing him twenty years before as 'the new kind of don; they give tutorials with a bottle of whisky by the armchair and a girl in the bedroom', and being so pleased at his marriage. His friends' affairs and intentions, honourable or otherwise, won his absorbed attention. He was ready with advice (if asked) and unoffended when it was not taken. All he asked was to be kept informed. 'Rosamund dining here last night assures me that you are to be married at any moment. I do not pay much attention to this but a word of news either way would be interesting.' And at another time when I did not know whether I was in love or infatuated he sent the only message that is of any use: 'Don't forget that your old friends are devoted to you and will stand by you no matter what you do.'

In Proust's final volume the enchanting, youthful creatures of the *belle époque* become in their middle and old age monsters unrecognisable as what they once were. So for a few of those whom Maurice created in the twenties – he created part of almost all his closest Oxford friends – he lost his lustre. They heard only the malice and forgot the generosity. They were offended by the coarseness and were no longer impressed by the enthusiasm for literature and scholarship. They contrasted the Maurice of their

youth with the post-war Warden: one of them called the latter
a noisy bore. The Warden was not in the strictest sense of the
word an intellectual – perhaps he never had been. In becoming
Warden some qualities atrophied: the delight in ideas for their
own sake – in ideas as distinct from conceits – and the energy to
pursue them. The energy had now been diverted into other channels and with it went something that his older friends had
believed was inalienably his. The Attributes of the intellectual
are as jealous as the Muses of the arts: at the first sight of a rival –
in this case Influence which a Warden or Vice-Chancellor must
inevitably exercise – they decamp in disgust. The army of Maurice's
mind still appeared in magnificent array. On the right wing stood
all the power of his scholarship, on the left wing his genius for
personal relations which never deserted him and remained as
strong as ever; but in the centre the desire to dominate and lead
displaced purely intellectual pursuits and now emerged as the
co-ordinating force.

There was, too, a change in his order of battle. Before the war
he had led the vanguard of the Immoral Front. The term, invented
by himself, embraced all those of whom the smug Establishment
of the age of Baldwin disapproved – Jews, homosexuals, people
whom odd views, or way of life, or contempt for stuffiness made
disreputable. But in the post-war days he found himself *coincé*.
Should he spurn every opportunity and remain an outsider, iso-
lated, rejected and rejecting? Or should he modulate, and use the
eminence and power which now were his to further the cause of
emancipation? In fact once he became Warden he had no choice;
the only free intellectual is he who evades all responsibilities and
executive duties and remains as uncommitted in the world of
action as he is committed in the world of ideas. Bowra was by
nature a poacher and he disliked having to draw on the velveteen
breeches of the gamekeeper. He mourned his youth. He once pulled
out his wallet to show me a photograph of himself when he was
young, and I noticed the quizzical, amused, sensual mouth. The
bull-dog had once been an engaging bull-terrier.

For one whose morality could hardly be said to be modelled on
the high values propagated by the Georgian public school, he was
highly competitive. He used to criticise Evelyn Waugh for deni-
grating the worth of any other writer or the success of his friends,
but Maurice himself was not free from envy. Out of his letters

peered the green-eyed monster when he mentioned Isaiah Berlin. Here was an old disciple, famous in America and wooed by the organisers of international gatherings; the foremost historian of ideas in this country who wrote in a powerful idiosyncratic style, the living embodiment of his personality and mind, a vehicle which was a reproach to Maurice's own inability to let himself go in prose; a man with the entrée to any society yet willing to give time to humble and obscure scholars whom Maurice would have dismissed as bores; more able than he, when the warm breezes of adulation from the world fanned him, to preserve the kernel, an ice-cube of his integrity. I noticed that when one invited the other to dinner Isaiah would propitiate his mentor and allow Maurice to dominate the stage by joining the auditors. It cost Maurice much to write his letter of congratulation when Isaiah received the O.M. The bile rose; but to give in to such a base emotion would be despicable; so he choked it down. On the other hand he never bottled up asperities about his friends nor remembered that, though one friend might genially shake with laughter when gouged, another might suffer and regard his quips as life-diminishing barbs. Yet both Isaiah and Roy Harrod (to whom he was bound by long, deep friendship) wrote noble eulogies of him; and indeed such was his power to create people and make them catch a glimpse of promise in themselves they had not known was there, that gratitude effaced resentment. Isaiah Berlin bound up his wounds, did not forget what he owed to Maurice in the thirties and, even when respect for Maurice as an intellectual had gone, something remained – love remained. Maurice, for his part, nursed his bruises, caused by his friend's refusal to dissemble and find a word of praise for his books, and chose Isaiah as the friend above all to whom he could speak about his despair and appeal for comfort.

Friendship means comfort: for grief, unhappiness and fear. Those at Oxford who knew Maurice best believed him to be secretly unhappy in the years after the war. Great talkers use talk as an opiate. An opiate for what? For the returning pain of failure to achieve what could or ought to be achieved; of the ruses used to deceive and cover up the failure; of the fear of exposure, shame, blackmail, death. He met the death of friends with bluster: 'Heard of any amusing deaths lately?' He was not in any important respect like Samuel Johnson but you were often reminded of a Johnsonian trait. He teemed with inner doubts. Johnson, muttering, grimacing, touching every post along a street, breaking off a conversation to repeat a phrase in the Lord's Prayer, was eccentric to the verge of madness. Maurice was not, but he had his manias. He had money-dick: constantly referred to the expense of existence; and once told me that he had warned A. L. Rowse, whose earnings from academic activities were to that historian a source of pride, that he could not afford to become Warden of All Souls. Blackmail haunted him: one of his oldest friends was ruined by blackmailers. Some ridiculous incident would convince him that at any moment he might be exposed. I experienced little of this — my weekends and holidays with him were galas. But I remember once hearing him and Dadie Rylands each assess how great his failure in life had been and I wondered at all the misery which these two, who meant so much to others, endured.

'I will take you at your word and come for next weekend. No need to arrange any pleasures. Quiet talks and sincere silences, they are my line. I will arrive in the afternoon probably via London.' Unfortunately I was out when he eventually arrived and on my return found his suitcase and a card: 'Not a very warm welcome.' His visits had to be planned with care.

'Last December you murmured something about coming over to see the Greek play. I gather *Oedipus at Colonus* is all over — so no doubt you forgot about it or were busy with dear Raymond. I mention this merely to put things right in case Provost Sheppard holds it against me.'

Nothing would have induced me to take him once again to the Greek play. On the last occasion when he attended, he drew attention, shortly after the rise of the curtain, to the knees of the Chorus, and engaged those on either side in such brisk conversation that a cold message was delivered to me during the interval to keep him quiet or get him out. Entertainments which demanded silence, such as the play or concerts, were not festivities for him: they interrupted talk.

His talk was prodigious. The first time I remember it in full flood was in Cambridge in 1944. He arrived much pleased that

Alick Smith had been elected Warden of New College. 'The omens were excellent. Now, when I was elected Warden of Wadham there was a clap of thunder and Milne's wife committed suicide in the gardener's shed with a large saw. Took her five minutes. When Smith was elected, Bolt – a Fellow of the College – died. Next day his wife committed suicide in the gas-oven of the Warden's Lodgings. Discovered by Mrs Fisher. Yes, I should say the omens were tip-top.' From there he moved to the sad and shocking story of how Fr Ratcliff had been kept out of the Chair of Pastoral Theology (a Crown appointment) by cabals of wicked old dons, by Hebdomadal guile in bamboozling the Patronage Secretary, and by Brendan Bracken's scandalous intervention in a mood of darkest puritanism – and all because there had been a whisper which suggested that he was a man who devoted himself to *pastoral* duties. By the time this sinful plot on behalf of the Establishment had been unfolded, we were at dinner and hard on the pursuit of the incompatibility of love and sex. Maurice started from the premise that sex was inescapably in the head. He then expounded the extreme view that appurtenances were more seductive than the beloved. Whereas the rest of us maintained that a look, a twist in the hair, the set of the eyes, the expression of the mouth, the walk, the tilt of the hips, created the obsessions which were the snares, Maurice put forward fetishism as the animator and argued that the object was more important than the subject: white shorts, bloomers, plimsolls, gaslight, the Crystal Palace – these were examples of the objects which elicited lust. (Much quoting from Betjeman.) He maintained that at one time his friend Philip Ritchie's grey flannel trousers occupied his mind far more than Philip Ritchie. Why did one fall in love with people whose morality was repulsive? Why should cards, crooks and bad hats exert such stunning erotic force? Did vitality, good looks and panache compensate for loutish sensibilities and low habits? How could one ward off the curse of intellectuals in love – guilt?

From the horrors of guilt we passed to the rebuffs. Barbara Rothschild and Bob Boothby declared that they had never been rebuffed. Dadie Rylands and I said we spent much time avoiding rebuffs. Maurice said, 'I create rebuffs before I am rebuffed.' At this point the conversation turned back to the significance of smell in sex. Maurice all the time firing his poop guns, 'Noel feels things sin-deep . . . He's safe in the arms of Kleist.' Then it sud-

denly turned to religion and whether belief in propositions should
be regarded as important, Maurice veering between a penchant
for Buddhism to a declaration that, were he a Christian, he would
settle for sound Low Church views – personal intercession by the
Saviour and bathing in the copious, atoning Blood of the
Lamb.

Those weekends are indelible. Maurice would appear fully
dressed for breakfast always wearing a waistcoat. After breakfast
he might read poetry in a deliberately non-poetic voice – he hated
une voix dorée – but in a style which emphasised the metre and
rhythms. Much criticism of the poets too – at one point he introduced the game of classing them as in the Tripos. Goethe notably
failed to get a First: 'No: the Higher Bogus.' 'Maurice, we've
forgotten Eliot.' 'Aegrotat.' Further analysis of the character of
dons and their wives: 'Which of the Bilburys do you dislike
most? Take your time . . .' Suddenly he would be off on a conceit.
What was the quintessence of Wykehamist? Who could be said
to be 'Very Wok of very Wok'? Minute charting of the channels
through which the Winchester conscience drains. Was there suffi-
cient evidence to establish the emergence in the evolution of the
species of a Wykehamist thigh characterised by its massive girth
(examples cited: Crossman and Sparrow). You found that in
playing such games his wit illuminated not only the conceit which
took his fancy but human nature. Then away on an architectural
walk – if in Oxford, Keble and the Shelley Memorial were
favourites and he would air his suspicions about modern buildings:
'They are entirely made of some ghastly stuff called cladding.' Or
to drinks with some undergraduates. He always welcomed undergraduates. 'That was,' he wrote of a weekend at King's:

'as always, most enjoyable, full of incident and variety and
much illumined by the memory of Provost Sheppard's recent
bad behaviour. I liked the boys very much and felt that they are
nicer and cleverer than ours, which I did not feel two years or
so ago. I fear that Mr Murray will come to a bad end but I
expect much of the others. Tell them I have discovered fragments of a new Canaanite epic – no talking horses, alas, but a
good goddess who makes infamous propositions to a handsome
young man.'

After the lunch party, a constitutional, a siesta and books, until the evening got under way. If you were staying with him, he might read his latest verse after dinner in the drawing-room. It is the only place where I laughed so much that exhausted from sitting I had to lie on the floor and hold on hard.

To go on holiday with him was an experience. He was not one to tramp for thirty miles over mountains or bury himself in the country and vegetate waiting for Nature to heal. A holiday in the Mediterranean which combined art and the sea pleased him most. He had a talent for pleasure. His resilience as a traveller was beyond praise and no disaster, whether mechanical or human, could disturb his invariable good humour. He had ways of coaxing his friends back into equanimity: if you felt liverish and disinclined to eat, that was the occasion on which to go to a specially good restaurant. You set out in the morning to visit the galleries and churches, and Maurice had an ingenious system of points. According to the greatness, or it might be the inaccessibility, of the work of art, you obtained so many points, and when you had totalled fifty you were entitled to a drink. But disappointment had its reward. If, hot and expectant, you found a church or gallery closed, you got an additional ten points. If you tramped to a gallery in search of Greek vases and were rewarded with a display of neolithic shards you immediately got fifteen points. Climbing one sweltering morning the twelve vast staircases of the Palazzo Pitti ('Pity 'tis, 'tis true') we arrived at the top floor expecting to see the treasures of the Baroque age and were met with the deplorable spectacle of rows of paintings of the Risorgimento. 'Thirty points!' he boomed as he strode triumphantly through it. Italian primitives did not awaken his finer powers of discrimination. ('Too many Gaddis and Daddis.') He stalked masterpieces. But he was not a man to linger over his aesthetic experiences. He would approach the Michelangelo Holy Family, pause, regard it as if it were a recalcitrant colleague, deliver judgment, 'Greatest work of man', and plod along to the next. But mention a painting later in the day and he would nearly always make some comment about its spiritual or literary qualities. He must have visited some churches and galleries twenty or thirty times.

Yet when you were in a museum with him you felt that his mind was never really far from the Dickensian characters who peopled it. Faced with a row of busts of later Roman emperors, he paused in front of each and identified them, 'Last, Gow, Adcock, Stiggins . . .' and mysteriously the marble statues began to assume in one's mind the features of these scholars. We came to the end of a row where there was a bust whose face had been completely weathered away, except for the beard, into total anonymity. I thought he would be defeated. But no: 'Senior Fellow under the old Statutes.'

Bathing he greatly enjoyed. He would emerge, the short stumpy figure expectant, vast head, large paunch and a curiously twisted navel much in evidence. His dive into the sea resembled a deliberate assault upon the ocean as if he wanted to punish Poseidon. When the tidal wave had subsided he would be seen rising from the deep at the salute, looking like an admiral who had refused to go down with his ship. He swam apparently standing up and when passing another couple would pronounce with shameless clarity on their social origins: 'English LMC.' ENT was one of the eventualities which he did his best to avoid, but if he failed, the English at the Next Table soon knew about his feelings. Without being tyrannical he expected punctuality. One evening, after a long siesta, we had forgotten the time in bed, when, without a knock the door was flung open and Maurice appeared to summon us for the evening drink. 'Most satisfactory' was his comment and, after a cursory inspection, he retired to await our arrival.

'I create rebuffs before I am rebuffed . . .' You very soon learnt how raw his skin was. His letters speak of a world in which the Legions of Darkness are in perpetual warfare with the Children of Light. He saw university politics as a ceaseless struggle against the enemies of freedom, vitality and the intellect: they were the *bien-pensants*, the trimmers, the advocates of the sound and safe, not to mention clericals, technocrats and progressives. When you were with him the large Johnsonian face was for ever mobile, responding to your remarks, giving expression to his own, alight, amused, dominating. But one feature in his face never smiled: his eyes. They were pig's eyes, fierce, unforgiving, unblinking, vigilant. They were inspecting the enemy's dispositions. Lucid as his prose was, his universe was Heraclitan and Dionysiac.

'A very enjoyable meeting on Friday when everyone lost their tempers, and Boase made some enemies for life. It is most pleasant when one's enemies quarrel with each other. After several hours of fierce debate some minor pious resolutions were passed, and everyone went away scowling and hissing and murmuring under their breath.'

That was observation : but he would flare up when he believed that wrong was being done :

'The board of electors have made a disgraceful election of a young queen. He may refuse, in which case he will be replaced by a thin old queen. Middleditch behaved abominably and killed the only good candidate. I have always said he was a back-stabber, from the highest motives of course. Tuck was the Queen-maker throughout. The Bugger's Opera.'

Nor did Cambridge escape :

'Smallsoles throughout has behaved in a very offensive manner – superior, snarling, muttering, plaintive – all the stigmata of the Trinity don at his worst . . . Your Vice-Chancellor, the glittering fraud, Willink, is no better but there is only two years of him. He has the air of knowing the inner mind of the Cabinet and producing it with a mysterious air but of course he is always wrong . . . The Master of Balliol has been ill but unfortunately is getting better. Otherwise deaths have been poor for the time of year . . .'

University affairs were part of his pantomime in which there were demon kings, brokers' men, dragons and Malvolios who had to be worsted. A few years later the dragons might have turned into a pride of lions whom Maurice would praise. But when something occurred which he considered cruel or inhuman he exploded in wrath. 'I had you in mind,' he wrote to me once, 'when our old and, I hope, dying friend at that black reactionary college refused to see the parents of a suicided boy on the grounds that he was busy and anyhow did not know the boy.'

Knowing the boys meant much to him. Generations of his undergraduates knew him, and I remember the exhilaration of meeting him for the first time before the war when I was taken to his Sunday morning salon the year after I graduated. He sympathised with and civilised the young, and he was unexcelled in getting a tipsy bore out of the room before the boy knew what had happened. Nor did he lose his head in the mild disturbances at Oxford at the end of his days as Warden. One of his undergraduates libelled a don who demanded his expulsion. Maurice made him apologise, but refused. One did not send young men down for indiscretions. His obituarist recorded that when some undergraduates wanted to send their objections to the proctorial system to the Privy Council, Maurice met the objection 'Why should they?' with the simple retort: 'Because they are entitled to and because they want to.'

He cheered on his friends. In the old method of electing a Chancellor, now superseded, at Cambridge, a small caucus of Heads picked their man and presented it as a *fait accompli* for endorsement by the Regent House. When on this hardly crucial issue as a lone voice I asked in the Discussion whether one other name at least had been considered, I received a letter which explains how he saw such matters:

> 'I am delighted to hear of your gallant stand against the corrupt bosses and that awful Spens. Of course they will win, but they will have been rattled, which is very good for them and makes them much more ready to compromise next time. Mountbatten would have been excellent . . . now I rather hope Nehru is put up and gets in. Your shares must be very high with the *non-bien pensants*, whoever they are.'

On the other hand, he was not a party man and detested the hypocrisies of the Left concerning freedom no less than the power of the Right; and his comment on the *Lady Chatterley's Lover* case in which I appeared as a witness put the matter in perspective:

> 'Well done. It is good to see the old cause of dirt so well defended, and I admire you very much for your skilful arguments and even more for having been able to read and remember the book, which must have been rather a gruelling experience for you. I comfort myself with the thought that now I need never read it.'

It sounds a brutal voice. But the brutality was often assumed, a figure of speech, a vein in the Oxford marble which ran back to an early-nineteenth-century Dean of Christ Church, "Presence of Mind' Smith, so-called because, when an undergraduate, he related how he and a friend were in a skiff on the Thames when the friend fell into the river, clutched the side of the boat, and in his frantic attempts to haul himself back as they drifted towards the weir was about to capsize it. 'Neither of us could swim; if I had not with great presence of mind hit him on the hands with a boat-hook both of us would have been drowned.' And his wit resembled that of another Oxford Smith. In invention, rapidity, fancy, verbal virtuosity and in his flights into fantasy, he was the heir of Sydney Smith. There can be no higher praise.

Everyone at Oxford knew who was Vice-Chancellor when Bowra held the office. His entertainment was princely. 'Bowra. Champagne and strawberries. Three glasses', was Enid Starkie's grateful memory of one of his garden parties at which she appeared attired in Maurice's phrase 'in all the colours of the Rimbaud'. He knew what he wanted and set out to get it by exceedingly tough methods of university politics and by keeping the committees amused. He hated deviousness. Open opposition won his respect. Of one Oxford operator he wrote:

'He is a hard-boiled customer who is not afraid of making highly wounding remarks. I rather like him, as at least he is not cagey. He is against Edwin as he thinks him pernickety. In fact Edwin is very good indeed in the Chair. He is less good on some other committees as he is hopelessly honest – not really a fault. But I can see that he won't go down very well with the Tory clique.'

He was not indulgent to his successors:

'The Vice-Chancellor bumbles on, splitting infinitives until the floor is covered with them.'

Or of another:

'As Vice-Chancellor he has one great virtue. He does not in the least care what conclusions are reached on any matter.'

Or again :

'He does not now even read the papers for Council and gets
them all wrong. Just when we seem to be in sight of a decision
he goes into reverse and it all starts again.'

When he was in the chair his object was to get matters through
on the nod, and to do so he set his tank on course directly to the
objective and opened the throttle. He did not have much patience
with those who could not keep up with the pace at which he con-
ducted business.

'The same cannot be said for Boase, who makes bad blood
about my rapid handling of business. Naturally he is very slow
and does not understand what it is about. However, as he likes to
be on the winning side, he has made an error, as when the other
day he found himself in a minority of three on Council and was
much taken aback.'

He was no university reformer. When he heard of our plan at
Cambridge to abolish the system of admissions whereby each
College had its own separate policy and procedures, the despair
of schoolmasters, he declared that it was a splendid reform in
that it would enable Wadham to get an even better entry. But
when change was forced on the ancient universities by the emergence of an admissions system under U.C.C.A. he threw his weight
behind it. He once made a speech in which he said : 'The undergraduate suicide rate is higher than it ought to be.' What then
happened confirmed him in his view that public pronouncements
were an error: all the progressives in Oxford were on his doorstep
demanding instant action and a university psychiatric service. He
shied violently. Yet he kept things moving. Oliver Franks was not
the sort of man who could have become his intimate friend : but
he respected him as honourable and dispassionate, voted for him
to become Chancellor against Macmillan, and threw his weight
behind the Franks Report when it was published. He did so because
he thought most of its recommendations were wise, but he got
additional satisfaction in doing so because some of his enemies and
perverse friends did not fail to appear in their true colours.

His letters to me were full of Oxford politics : he thought little

E

of those who pontificated about the higher moral purpose of higher education. Nor, since at Oxford in those days the Vice-Chancellor held office for no more than three years, could he ever have taken over the role in the Vice-Chancellors' Committee played by the two brothers Charles Morris of Leeds and Philip of Bristol (irreverently nicknamed by Bowra after a music hall duo in the twenties as 'Toots and Lorna'). But in the ancient universities he was without a peer as an academic leader. At Cambridge there was no Vice-Chancellor or academic leader in the days of his influence to touch him, and the loss was immeasurable – in the level of distinction in making appointments and in the preparation of business in such a way as to make clear the implications of the different decisions which might be taken. When he retired, Oxford had moved into a new era with Council's power to lead and the Vice-Chancellor's capacity to bring affairs to the boil enhanced, yet without losing the essence of Oxford's democracy of dons.

Appointments were to him by far the most important issue in the university, and in this he was right. Appointments matter more than anything else – more than syllabuses, cost effectiveness, plot ratios, student load, and all the other terms of art with which scholars if they are to continue to run their affairs have to concern themselves. The right men – outstanding and productive scholars, devoted and stimulating teachers, men of originality and imagi-nation, open-hearted and magnanimous – are the life-blood of a university. But where are the paragons to be found? At the moment of choice the scrupulous quaver. Original, yes – but is he *sound?* Full of vitality, but a trifle too vulgar? Draws an audience, does he? – are we sure he is not a charlatan? A difficult man – hardly likely to be acceptable to our colleagues? And so the inoffensive and second-rate slip in.

Maurice was not a man to quaver. He cared deeply for scholar-ship, and whatever holes could be picked by experts in his own writings, he was a professional, hard-working and disciplined, who brought order and light to any subject he touched, quick to spot a dilettante or the bogus. He did not want light-weights. But still less was he prepared to put up with stolid and unimaginative pedants, the worthy men who unquestionably had made contri-butions to the subject but in doing so were helping to kill it. His methods did not endear him to those who like to weigh candidates in the balance as if they were bags of sugar, taking away a few grains or adding a few more in the vain attempt to get perfect equilibrium. He could be unscrupulous and twist the rules. If a rival candidate clearly had superior claims to his own, he would give way – but they had to be very clear. If votes were needed he set himself to collect them. 'Had all the votes lined up; everybody perfectly all right; took particular trouble with the mathematicians; mathematicians voted the wrong way.' His eyebrows shot up when one of them excused himself by saying that he had been convinced by the arguments. Maurice rarely allowed himself to be convinced by arguments. He had heard them all before and recognised the apparently artless comment as a well-worn trick of the trade. He mastered the arguments before he went into committee, made his judgment and expected his allies, if they had not the energy or wit to do so themselves, to trust him. But on occasions they stumbled away sore and saddened. For if it became clear that he would lose – and he was lightning-quick to sense how the votes would fall – he would switch to avoid defeat and loss of prestige, leaving his allies in disarray. You felt that in the French Revolution, Girondin though he was, he would somehow have survived the Terror and emerged as one of Napoleon's marshals, not by guile but by speed of manoeuvre.

There were bad appointments as well as good in his day – as indeed there must always be when future achievement is impossible to forecast and the choice so often lies between settling for a limited but tangible output and gambling on the sample in a small core, which may well prove deceptive, as evidence of a hidden gold-mine. But able though he was in marshalling support for his man, he put scholarship before personal friendship. He was fond of Enid Starkie, but he rightly judged that as a scholar she was not in the same league as Jean Seznec: in the election to the Professorship of French she lost by one vote and Maurice's letter of comfort to her was sensitive and truthful. Where he excelled was as a tireless spotter of talent in fields far from his own. Many young scholars owed much to his encouragement and promotion – among them some of the most able and gifted today. He used to tell me that he always looked for vitality and strength of character and that it was as easy to be dazzled by signs of brilliance as it was to be over-impressed by quantity of published work.

Where appointments were concerned, confidentiality was a

convention to be dismissed from the mind. Even if he were not on the board of electors he could be guaranteed to be relaying without compunction the story of the proceedings within forty-eight hours and details of all the manoeuvres, intrigues and votes cast attributed personally. Those such as Tommy Balogh who maintained that the proceedings of all appointments committees should be open, had nothing to complain of if Maurice was involved; at Cambridge, however, where we practised discretion, we shivered when the prattle of some Oxford economist after an election led to the recriminations which confidentiality is supposed to obviate . . . This breezy indiscretion was much appreciated by his correspondents.

> 'Much trouble here finding a Head for St Antony's College. £2,000 a year, plus £300 for entertainment, nothing at all to do – will anyone take it? Not they! It is hawked around and gets blank refusals. Sparrow was approached and turned it down on the grounds that he could not make up his mind to accept it – refined but circular, I feel.'

No man relished more the niceties of contested elections:

> 'The All Souls elections were dull. They elected two men from Magdalen – one of whom is going to be a parson, the other a psychoanalyst. The atheists voted against the first, the papists against the second, so Warden Sparrow held the scales and had his way. He seems to have conducted the proceedings in a masterly manner.'

To anyone outside a university the frenzy which elections and appointments produce inside it seem petty and absurd. People enjoy hearing of fulminating accusations of bad faith, betrayal, jobbery and dishonesty darkening the air of common rooms, which echo to the sound of the sharpening of knives. Yet those who work within them know that without some tension the best men and women will not get appointed. 'Pity about him,' Maurice once said of a recently elected Head of House. 'Can't get worked up about the appointment of the new chaplain.'

His style of life before the war made some of the more austere and eminent classical scholars regard him as a centre of deadly contagion. Gilbert Murray, whom he revered, liked but disapproved of him. The Germans, so I am told, dismissed him; and when Fraenkel, the most learned classical scholar of his generation, came to Oxford as a refugee, they did not comprehend each other and Fraenkel's contempt hurt. Some enemies called him a charlatan – that was trash; others said he lacked thoroughness – that was true. Nor was he the kind of scholar who sets himself painfully to discover new methods of teaching his material, thus enabling him to transform his subject. He was accused of lacking integrity, and in discussing topics he too often resembled a circus performer jumping off the back of one horse and on to another. In conversation he could fleer and veer. I have seen him hurtle along the down-line crushing a reputation on the way and then, aware of silent disapproval among one or more of his auditors, switch into a siding, change tracks and career back on the up-line steaming praise. It seemed not to cross his mind that someone might think this cowardly or dishonest. Intellectuals may not regard loyalty to people as highly as other men, but they are rightly suspicious of those who seem not to be loyal to those things which bring order to life – to principles, judgments, and abstract propositions which are won only by hard work and at a cost. Company could tarnish him: he liked to be liked – he wanted terrifyingly to be liked. It is a fault. But in the silence of his study he did not lack integrity. The lucid statements, unobscured by weasel-words or ambiguities, never left his reader in doubt about what he thought. He came to recognise how best he could use his gifts and he was never wiser than when he widened his field of scholarship and used his gift for language to explore the European poetic tradition.

In his public life he presented a splendid paradox. His friends blenched when he elbowed aside opposition or went back on his tracks; his enemies fumed and stamped indignant at their treatment. But at Oxford, or indeed at any institution with which he was connected, spirits shot up when he was in action. He outshone everyone, his very existence in a place doubled its energy, its vitality, its gaiety. He had the extraordinary gift of making people feel that life was more exciting, more full of possibility, adventure, depth, comedy and poignancy than they had dreamt possible. His disillusioned friends felt this. So, more astonishingly, did his enemies and detractors. The very fact that he was full of frailties (never absurdities) – that he was impulsive and governed by passionate emotions – put heart into his colleagues. The occupational hazard of being a don is to become anaemic, and an hour with Bowra was like a blood transfusion. Indeed he resembled a fine commander of troops. You knew that using every stratagem he would fight for his men and be prepared to evade or even disobey orders from above; you might disapprove of him but you could not deny that he would scrounge, high-jack and brow-beat so that his show should have every advantage. Ultimately his loyalty embraced them all, the devoted and doubters alike. Using the word in its time-honoured sense, he was beyond doubt or challenge the greatest don of his generation.

Beyond all else he was a don. By all accounts his first visit to Harvard was more agreeable to him than his second. He was proud to have been invited to hold the Charles Eliot Norton Chair and in later years making a speech said that it was something to have been Professor of Poetry at Oxford, Eng., and Professor of Poetry at Cambridge, Mass. 'If anyone here can boast of being Professor of Poetry at Cambridge, Eng., and Professor of Poetry at Oxford, Mississippi, let him stand up in his shame.' But in 1948 he shared the common English resentment of American power, foresaw the excesses of the anti-communist forces, and found President Conant's conception of a university not his own. At one point he wrote asking for food parcels to be sent to him from England.

'This life here is pretty dismal and I live like the Stoic wise man – two small rooms, over-heated and underfurnished. The food is bad beyond description: breakfast – cold pancakes with syrup on them: luncheon and dinner – stew with vegetables boiled for weeks until they are like the food one gives to chickens. One gets a good meal in Boston but it's not near and costs the devil. I flew to California for Christmas to stay with my old friend, Ernst Kantorowicz. It was very agreeable as he knows no Americans and has collected some very eccentric Russians. He is also a very good cook indeed and does wonderful things with flaming brandy over ducks stuffed with truffles. The dons here are very persecuted – the lower dons starved and over-worked, sacked without reason at a moment's notice and compelled to lecture on subjects of which they know nothing. I have made some friends among these untouchables and they are devoted to me. I hear that

George's old friend, Conway, has just died. He had recently married a tart who had quite a name for killing husbands.'

He enjoyed visits to the *beau monde*. Lunches and dinners at Ann Fleming's and Pamela Hartwell's gave him pleasure, but the fashionable world, still less the world of fashion, was not a place he was tempted to inhabit. 'Undoubtedly right, certainly, certainly,' he boomed, as in his old age Marcelle Quinton expounded the art of buying day clothes at Hartnell's precisely because it was renowned for evening dresses: the secrets of *haute couture* remained mysterious. In his youth, so I believe, he had courted Bloomsbury and aristocrats. Both had repulsed him, and he neither forgot nor forgave (he once referred to E. M. Forster's work as a wedding-cake left out in the rain.) Aristocratic bewilderment at his conversational gambits made him ill at ease and he could lose his nerve and appear to suck up. In fact he had no desire to get in with them. More to the point he was contemptuous of anyone in his circle who courted the rich in café society. For him they represented a special Gehenna of boredom and falsity, and it seemed unthinkable that anyone would voluntarily expose themselves to such vapid conversation and mindless company. Eccentrics were more to his taste. He loved John Betjeman for delighting in their company: they were to him a proof that human nature was unpredictable and untamable by the lawgivers and the technocrats.

He genuinely loathed the Establishment. He thought their values and politics corrupt. But, like numbers of people, Maurice could not bear to renounce totally the gifts and places which the world which he rejected had to bestow. No call came in the Second World War, and even after his successful Vice-Chancellorship his name did not feature on those lists which circulate in Whitehall of possible chairmen of government committees. If he suspected that someone was oiling, he would be alluded to as 'winning golden opinions all round': one don, who was winging his way to Vice-Chancellorships, was described as 'a go-getting slug'. Sometimes he would be tempted to retreat from an advanced position in order to propitiate these deities. There was said to have been one fearful occasion when Enid Starkie put Gide up for an honorary degree and asked Maurice to have him to stay at the Warden's Lodgings: Maurice panicked and said he would have nothing to do with it, much to the chagrin of his friends who did not believe that the presence of the *maître* in Wadham, however notorious his homosexuality, would in any way impair Maurice's reputation, never high with the ultra-respectable at any time. The blackmail mania was at work. (His essay on Cavafy contains no reference to the fact that one-third of Cavafy's poems are about homosexual love.) What kept him out of national affairs was not lack of flexibility or even excess of emotion in committee but the fear inspired by his unbridled tongue outside committees. One of his contemporaries, who had risen to high places in the service of the State, once spoke to me contemptuously of Maurice's public advocacy of liberal causes as an indication of immaturity and of donnish ignorance of how the world worked. Maurice would have replied that he knew only too well how the world worked and, like Byron, knew how to recognise a time-server or a tyrant when he saw one. His conception of liberty was not utilitarian. It was Byronic.

As he grew older he yearned for praise. Sitting next to Queen Frederica of Greece àt lunch in the embassy when his friend, the poet George Seferis, was ambassador, he was told by the Queen how odious Royalty found flattery. 'Really, ma'am?' I heard Maurice say, 'I can't get enough of it.' His craving for honours was voracious. It was not simple snobbery, nor his resentment at the decoration of the undeserving, nor mean-mindedness. It came in part from a natural desire to show his seniors, the Old Gang, who thought he smelt of brimstone, that they could not keep him out. Was the great stodge of able complacent people going to exclude him and, while pretending to shuffle the pack, turn up all the familiar-face cards? Isaiah Berlin believed his obsession with honours a sign that his self-confidence had been fatally impaired by that insidious influence at Oxford, his philosophy tutor H. W. B. Joseph. If he could only pile up honours and set them beside the ever-lengthening line of his books, if he could construct out of them a palisade, a barricade, then surely, then at last, his reputation would be beyond challenge. Both greater and lesser men have become a prey to such fantasies : and indeed the hunger to acquire hoods and medals is not as rare as all that in academic life.

In fact he did not do all that badly. His honorary doctorates multiplied. His peers elected him President of the British Academy. The fact that he was made a Knight before he was Vice-Chancellor, showing that he had been honoured for his scholarship and not for his skill as an administrator, gave him particular pleasure; and when other Vice-Chancellors or high academic administrators were similarly rewarded he enjoyed analysing their scholarly achievements. 'They say he once had something to do with agriculture.' He set store on the letters of congratulation he received – and did not receive. When he was elected Professor of Poetry at Oxford he wrote:

'I am only too pleased to sit in the chair of Arnold, Bradley, Ker, Mackail, etc., and hope to raise the level from that of my predecessor, a deplorable clergyman. The campaign was very enjoyable and C. S. Lewis was outmanoeuvred so completely that he even failed in the end to be nominated and I walked over without opposition. Very gratifying to a vain man like myself.'

When his name appeared in the New Year's Honours as a Knight he replied:

'Thank you for your telegram. It was clever of you to spot the news between the nightclubs. It was all very gratifying and I make no attempt to hide my pleasure. As you know, I have had my full share of persecution mania and this has dealt it quite a blow. I am much enjoying the obvious discomfiture of enemies. Poor Cross, who is a martyr to envy, tried to be nice in his letter but did not really succeed. Stiggins has not written and nor has Fraenkel – all is as it should be.'

The high German decoration, *Pour le Mérite*, given in the past to Thomas Carlyle and Bernard Shaw, comforted him in old age. He stood there in the Embassy, surrounded by the guests, many chosen by him, whom the Ambassador had kindly invited. As an eminent German scholar made a speech in his praise, he looked as if he were facing a firing squad while the sentence of death was being read to him. In the event he was not shot but nearly garrotted, as it was only after a struggle that the ribbon could be got over his massive head and round the stalwart neck. But after Frau Dr Lohmeyer had run round him several times heaving first from this angle and then from that, the medal eventually ended up under his left ear. One final pleasure awaited him. Staying with us over the last Christmas he was to see, he told me that he had received the customary letter inviting him to become a Companion of Honour but could not convince himself that there had not been a mistake and he would receive a message to the contrary. Later he wrote:

'It has come through and is in *The Times*. Last night I foresaw last minute intervention but there was no need . . . Any sane man likes to have his work recognised, and Aristotle was right when he said that honour was the greatest of external goods.'

Exasperated by her adopted country, Lydia Keynes once said that Englishmen were either boys or old boys. Maurice was both. He was an immensely masculine bisexual, but no exponent of the art of chatting up girls: when with them he had not much instinct for what they were thinking or feeling. One recalled the judgment which one of John Oliver Hobbes's characters, Lady Theodosia, passes on her niece: 'She was born for noise, not love.' But he did fall in love. I had heard in the days before I knew him the story of his engagement to a girl whose troubled mind became seized with mighty dread: so she consulted Bob Boothby – a man of some experience in such matters. 'I feel as if I am being whirled dizzy on a merry-go-round revolving at eighty miles an hour. What shall I do?' 'Jump off,' said Bob. Perhaps most of all he loved Joan Eyres-Monsell, and during the post-war years Barbara Warner, Elizabeth Bowen, Penelope Betjeman, Iris Murdoch, Baroness von Wangenheim (whom he rescued from Germany) and Elsie Butler at Cambridge had a special relationship with him. He liked girls to join his weekend parties for lunch or dinner: they were often good-looking but generosity and audacity were the qualities in girls which he particularly admired. Feminine vagaries, wiles, stratagems, and bad behaviour intrigued him: one of his favourite characters in literature, whom he said he was always recognising in real life, was Cleopatra. 'A pi tart' he would say. The most reckless girls sexually, he would declare, were also gifted with the greatest power of self-deception, and as mothers ferocious in the protection of their children. His analysis could be deadly. He described one enslaved girl as a 'mouse at bay'. Another, the very reverse, was christened 'the meringue-outang'.

I know nothing except by hearsay of his own experiences. By the time I knew him he appeared to hold the position of non-playing captain. He may still have put himself on to bowl occasionally, for he sent me an account which suggested that he retired hurt. I once received a lament:

'But she brought Sebastian with her which meant no fucking and, much worse, his presence. He is indescribably awful, positively and dynamically fourth-rate – he sings, whistles, never stops talking, is infinitely pretentious and ignorant, not at all respectful, physically hideous and is embarrassing to be seen with! I behaved like an angel and had only one very small tiff with him – no one can say that I am not a saint! Why the old girl likes him I can't imagine but it is obviously no use being nasty to him – that only makes her more protective about him. God preserve me from gigolos!'

'*Zwei Seelen wohnen, ach! in meiner Brust.*' Like Reynolds' portrait of Garrick, the spirit of Comedy pulled him by the arm, while Romantic Tragedy summoned imperiously. The comedy of encounters in bed inspired his finest flights but his vision of love was Romantic. One of his conceits consisted of drawing a line across the northern hemisphere, everywhere south of which was the sex zone, everything north of which the drink zone. The line ran north of Provence, Italy, Greece and Persia, thence to the Himalayas, north of China, south of Japan and dived south to the Mexican border. ('America? Drink zone pretending to be sex.') The people in the sex zone might well live in countries where wine was grown, and might even have strict sexual conventions; but for them sex was associated with happiness, gratification, enjoyment – a necessity in life to be luxuriantly indulged with either boys or girls, a delight associated with gaiety and never with remorse. In all Cupid's pageant there was no monster – except one, Death, feared and detested as the great annihilator. Conversely the people in the drink zone could not come to terms with sex. Sex was acknowledged as a force of overwhelming power – what people produced more talented and ingenious practitioners than the Germans? But in the drink zone sex was cursed with guilt, darkness, despair, complexity. So far from men fearing death, the death-wish lay heavy upon them. When Siegfried spoke of *leuchtende Liebe, lachender Tod* he was asserting that redemption after the disasters brought about by passion could be achieved only through death after love.

While he loved the Mediterranean, Bowra did not take his *jeu d'esprit* all that seriously. He had nothing in common with that generation of dons and writers which preceded his own and was so mawkish and sentimental in its idealisation of Greek and Italian pagan morality. He saw as many connections as divisions between Greek drama and the Romantic movement. Men and women in love were possessed by a *daimon*. Infatuation led to self-deception; self-deception to delusion; and delusion to misfortune and calamity. When the tempest stove in the life-boats and smashed the vessel against the rocks, you could if you chose apportion blame: but to do so was irrelevant. Cataclysmic forces beyond human control tossed men and women about. To fail to recognise the existence of these forces was to turn your back on the insights of the Romantic movement and to ignore the sombre utterances of the poets of antiquity. His sense of ridicule was too acute for him to subscribe to any inflated Romantic theory about passion, but equally his sense of the grand style, his warm-bloodedness, his dedication to a vision in which human beings felt, instead of being imprisoned by good form, made him hostile to cold-hearted sex. Much of his verse was a satirical commentary on the sexual morality of his world.

John Sparrow once wickedly said that it was a pity that Maurice had cut himself off from posterity: his prose was unreadable and his verse was unprintable. Whether or not he was released in his verse from his inhibitions, it is certainly unsurpassable in the vigour, candour and fantasy with which it describes sexual activity; and if any hedonist among scholars in the next century decides (improbably) to compile the equivalent of the Greek Anthology for our age, Bowra's verses would find a place as scabrous and satirical successors to Meleager and Leonidas. It is as if Maurice passed beyond the atmosphere confining his own personality and soared weightless into outer space. Each poem usually echoes one by Yeats, Hardy, Kipling or some other model. Some are exercises in pure parody and have nothing to do with sex, such as the three All Souls election songs or this esoteric Yeatsian mist:

> Profound Goronwy thought it out
>   That on the farthest star,
> Where Farquharson lives out his dreams
>   In timeless avatar,

The bobbins of the world go round
  Alone with Dr Parr.

Von Hügel heard the legend told
  By wise budgerigar,
That on Ben Adam's holy mount
  No wind of thought can mar
Such flow of sweetness as I find
  Alone with Dr Parr.

The heterosexual verse is usually of singular savagery and invention, paeans to the goddesses of fertility, lust and potency. They
often celebrate his friends' activities. 'Oh dear,' he wrote once
in commiseration, 'what are the pains of normalcy!' There were
pains too in homosexuality. He did not view all the activities
of the Homintern with benign equanimity. Someone as masculine
as he had little patience with old sissies and he lampooned their
advances rather in the style of an Andy Warhol movie:

When the dusk has descended,
  He wanders afar;
And enjoys a gay tussle
  With Jolly Jack Tar.

Or expounds to stout guardsmen
  The claims of Cézanne;
He knows all the ways
  Of a man with a man.

Where else in the world
  Can such graces be seen?
Our greatest, our only
  Philosopher-queen!

His longest exploration of the horrors, hysteria and humiliations
of being an active homosexual is made in a parody of Eliot, a
Waste Land of the life of one of his oldest friends, Adrian Bishop,
a large, florid figure, who had been his contemporary but at King's.
Maurice used to speak of his relationship to Adrian much as Sher-
lock Holmes used to speak of his brother Mycroft, namely as some-

one who was more inventive, more amusing, more fantastical with greater power over words, greater skill in punning, greater fecundity in outrage and literary allusion, and visited more frequently by the Muses than he himself: and who, but for calamity and indolence, would have overtaken Maurice. So notorious were Adrian's homosexual escapades that he lost his job in an oil company, was expelled from several countries, was blackmailed on several occasions and was rescued from the gutter in Berlin by Maurice. During the thirties he had taken vows and entered a monastery, and assumed the name of Brother Thomas. On the outbreak of war he asked his abbot to release him from his vows, and turned up at King's in 1940 on one of those extraordinary army courses invented during the period of the phoney war for officers who, it was supposed, would govern a supine Germany – which Adrian having spent several uninhibited years in Berlin in Weimar days was supposed to be qualified to do. When this wonderfully gifted and charming man fell off a balcony at his hotel in Teheran when engaged in intelligence duties there, and was killed, Maurice wrote a threnody upon his life and on the lives of all the homosexuals in the twenties. It was called *Old Croaker*, and here are the first two sections:

I

Oh, stark, stark, stark amid the blaze of June
    Uncoveredly stark,
With broad black hips, artificially sunburnt
    And rubicund lips that challenge the tomato.
Brown shorts, brown necks, that encumber the Métro
    Sidelong glances down Unter den Linden.
Barönin Grossartig, of a first-rate family,
    Said to be the fattest woman in Europe,
Went to bed with a dud Czech,
    Who talked French with a real French accent.
    He froze all her assets
And the psychologist takes over her guilt-edged securities.

    I will arise and go now and go to have a pee
        Way down in Innisfree
        That's where I wish to be

With a corporal on my knee.
     Oh, is it town or gown or touzled hair
A touzled boy-scout's hair
     Inside the W.C.?

        Over the Wannsee
         The saxophone
        Plays How do you do, do
         Mister Brown?
    An evzone with harmonica
      In a ginshop once I saw
    Leonidas, a Spartan lad,
      And was he eager to be had,
        Or was he?

He laid his dentures carefully on the shelf,
Lifted his skirts up just to give a peep
And in sublime oblivion of self
Began to snore in regimental sleep . . .
Goldstein is in Bohème or Silhouette,
His cigarette-case of synthetic jade,
He cautiously selects the best tapette
Who is still overworked if underpaid.

His Schaumwein bubbles in a lalique glass
From which an aphrodisiac peeps out.
He makes a nicely calculated pass
And Putzi understands what he's about.
The bar attendant orders drinks all round,
The tango summons to the dancing-floor,
The last train passes on the underground—
He slips behind the lavatory door . . .

Little Jack Horner
Sat in Cosy Corner
Pretending to be pi
  Asked me to take him for a honeymoon in Venice
To the Vierjahreszeiten with Wystan Auden.
Kennen Sie Christopher Isherwood?
Of course I just live for Art and Music . . .

Lead blindly tight amid the revolving room:
I'm tight and stark, and fed up, far from home.
Das ist die Liebe der Matrösen
      O maisons! Ó gâteaux!
Je cherche un matelot
      You called me baby-doll a year ago.
But Dr Faulkner in the heather-bloom
Blindly explores the owner's sitting room,
      Minus Thirteen eludes the closet door
And leaves his Abendessen on the floor.

          At Hyde Park Corner
          The buses stop.
          Her Majesty's Forces
          Like a drop.
          Miles in the singular
          Common and supine
          But the plural cases
          Are always masculine.

    I want to go back, I want to go back,
    I want to go back to my bed.
    With Faivre cachet in my head.

At Spandau then I came.

Prevent us, O Lord, prevent us
      In all our wooings.

II

Because there is no cash but only credit,
Because there is no credit but only credit
Because there is no cash,
Because it is more blessed to give than to take
I will not give but forgive,
Take and not forsake,
Take what is yours and ours, for our, your sake
Lord grant us to forgive
Those who do not take but give,
Forgive us our creditors as we forgive
Their credit against us.

... Prey on us now and in the hour of our debts

At the first vision of his golden hair
Would you not suddenly turn and stare?
Stand at the corner, light a cigarette,
Pretend your thoughts were neither here nor there,
Remark that the weather is neither fine nor wet,
Step upon orange-peel or banana-skin,
Ready to take part in a tennis set,
Go roller-skating in the Winter Garden,
Take lessons on the piano or mandolin,
Help his old mother take the washing in.

> There is no alcohol in the soda-fountain
> But only soda.
> Give a Pernod to the poor old Guy
> Where is the Fernet Branca that I bought
> To share in Paris with a mobled queen?

The Korn King's court is empty, the Dantziger Goldwasser
>   Stands on the counter unopened.
At the Tour d'Argent the duck is not what it was.
>   Put on the lights and then put on the lights,
That's the worst of these cheap cars.
>   What have I done to deserve all this?
What have I done?
>   Poor Tom's a-cold.
Prevent us, O Lord, in all our wooings ...

The springs that fed his verse were numerous, some of them peculiar, but the most powerful was his own passion for poetry. It is true that his prose was flat. It is true that he was an interpreter, rather than a critic, of poetry. It is true that he ignored the revolution in criticism during the twenties at Cambridge which was, perhaps, that university's most striking contribution to the study of the humanities between the wars. But when the customary reservations about his workaday methods have been made, his achievement in relating the greatest poets of modernism in France, Germany, Italy, Greece, Russia, Spain, Ireland and in this country is without parallel or challenge, especially when set beside his work on primitive and literary epic. In October 1946 Seferis referred to

F

him in his diary as 'one of the few Europeans still left in Europe.
He has an intimate knowledge of poets from Pasternak to Lorca',
and Bowra quite independently referred to Seferis as 'a splendid
gloomy European figure'. Nothing as authoritative on modernism
in European poetry had appeared before Bowra's *The Heritage
of Symbolism* and its sequel *The Creative Experiment*. The only
precursor was Edmund Wilson's *Axel's Castle*. Yet the mention
of Edmund Wilson must make one pause. For here Bowra's limitations as a critic and intellectual rise to mind. Edmund Wilson
was quirky, erratic and, when for instance writing on the Dead Sea
scrolls, no more than a journalist. But if we ask which of the two
explored the literature and culture of their times to greater effect
there can be but one answer. There was an heroic cast to Wilson's
thoroughness, he went at his material with greater intensity, he
would go to all lengths and pains to master his sources and to
distinguish reality from appearance. The struggle lay only partially
concealed beneath the readable, persuasive prose. What is more
Wilson, as a fine critic must, dug into himself to find the answers.
You can sense the granite of his sensibility splintering as he drilled
it to discover how far the strata had shifted under the impact of
the work of art. Little of this prodigious energy emerges in Bowra's
criticism, industrious and able though it is. Yet one should never
forget the debts contracted when one is young. Published during
the war, Bowra's works on modern poetry first introduced me to
Valéry and Stefan George whom I had never read, and gave me
some notion for the first time of what Rilke was about. I knew
nothing of Blok: now I knew something. Bowra's anthology of
translations of Russian poetry was another book of utmost importance to me. I learnt far more from Bowra's books than I did from
Wilson. It may be that if I had been much older and had read more
widely I would not have felt the same. But my gratitude for these
books remains with me to this day.

Maurice could not be for me what he was to my near-contem-
poraries at Oxford. For them he was a great liberator, the leader
of the movement against the *funeste* and soft-spoken philistine
conformity. He had known them as undergraduates or as young
Fellows and watched over their destinies. I was grown up by the
time I knew him well. But if he was not crucial to the development
of my character, he was crucial to my spiritual health. You could
not know him without recognising his total allegiance to learning

and poetry. If he was not among the great creative scholars of his times – and only a handful at any one time can be so described – he was an immensely learned man, and he made you feel ashamed of your ignorance and slovenliness. The range of his reading challenged your own provinciality and sloth. In the post-war years he was always suggesting that one should read poets whom the new orthodoxy had dismissed as negligible or harmful – Tennyson, Swinburne, Kipling. He did not misjudge their achievement: much of Swinburne he would say was meaningless. But he determined to demonstrate what they had achieved. If he was not someone, such as George Rylands or Isaiah Berlin, who had only to discuss a topic to give me some new insight, he was a traveller forever suggesting that if only you would journey further some new and life-enhancing experience was yours for the asking.

His oldest friends, such as Sylvester Gates, mattered most to him, but he came inevitably to rely more on the younger as the years passed. When you asked how old someone was, Maurice would often reply in Wade-Gery's phrase: 'Our age.' This concept described anyone who came up to Oxford or Cambridge from 1919 to, I would judge, 1952. At that point the cultural climate began to change, and I have the impression that with the exception of certain young dons in his own College (of whom perhaps the last was Philip Lloyd-Bostock), he relied for companionship on 'our age'. For our age he was an arbiter, a barometer of our behaviour. Deep-seated as was his hatred of injustice and cruelty, the rule of life by which, so it seemed to me, he set most store was to read poetry, to live by it and with it, to turn to it for wisdom, to pray that it would continue to replenish the springs of feeling which flow ever more sluggishly the older one gets, and above all to reverence the poets as men, like Pushkin's prophet, on whose tongue a burning coal had been laid. Not only dead poets, but the living exponents of the European heritage. You realised that beneath the noise and the laughter, the peppering of targets and the fountains, was the conviction that unless you refreshed yourself by re-reading the poets and letting them, if only for an hour or so, take command, you would inevitably become a castrated pedant or a dehumanised bureaucrat – and beyond redemption.

This was part of his religion; what the other parts were I do not know. What did he believe? 'Looking forward to meeting God. Got six questions to put to Him. UNANSWERABLE.' But then, cold belief was not to him the substance of religion: it was a mere attribute. Just as he held the old-fashioned notion that poets were inspired, so people's beliefs seemed to him to be a poor guide to their spiritual state. This scepticism about propositions had two consequences. Dogmatic Christianity with all the meaning that it had for John Betjeman or Evelyn Waugh was beyond him. But so was a rationalist interpretation of being: atheism or earnest agnosticism seemed to him to be mechanistic, brittle, superficial, cold, and to exclude so much of experience as to be unworthy of a serious man's attention. As a classical scholar he drew his religion, so it seemed to me, from ancient Greece and Rome. If he could hardly claim much of a reputation for *gravitas*, he had his full share of *pietas*. The gods must be given their due, and by humble rituals he showed that he did not forget them. When he entered a Roman Catholic church, he would march to the font and cross himself. In this he certainly surpassed Dr Johnson's friend, Campbell, who had never been in a church for many years but always pulled his hat off when he passed one: indeed he scarcely ever missed Chapel at Wadham. In his Oxford, so dominated by philosophy, so dedicated to the discovery of the truthfulness of propositions and the niceties of belief, his conception of religion appeared strange. But it would not have seemed strange to a modern Greek who lives in a country where a child cannot go to school unless he has been baptised, where Easter is celebrated with gusto in the churches and where intelligent and cultivated people, whose views on the eternities are not to be supposed to be all that different from other Europeans, cheerfully accept the rituals of the Orthdox Church and will burn a candle in front of an ikon like the humblest.

Maurice used to explain his actions by saying that he wanted only to be polite: but there was in him a desire to propitiate and placate, almost a plea for forgiveness. It was as if, like a conquering Roman general of old mounted in the chariot during his Triumph, he heard the slave whispering in his ear that he was mortal. The congregation at his funeral found themselves improbably singing *Lead Kindly Light*, and the line 'I loved the garish day and, spite of fears, Pride ruled my will', was not the kind of penitential self-humiliation which he inflicted upon himself. But *hubris* and *nemesis* were often in his thoughts. His splendid exuberance, his irrepressible vehemence, his razor-sharp sense of the ridiculous and his overwhelming drive could have made him degenerate into a dictatorial, overbearing bully. The memory of what the gods do to the great and powerful, however well-intentioned they may be, kept him in check. The poet he revered most was Homer; and he did not forget the passage where Achilles is reminded by his old tutor that prayers are the daughters of Zeus who, if a man rejects them, see that Infatuation is sent to harm him and make him pay the penalty. Unlike Achilles Maurice gave the daughters of Zeus the honour due to them.

'Dear Dawkins died very nicely in front of the college. He fell down in the street and was off to eternity. As he lay there he looked like a schoolboy, with all the wrinkles gone and a beatific smile on his face, the crutch flung aside. A nice end and may I have one like it.'

The gods heard his prayer.

7

John Betjeman

A Formative Friend

Stand with me on a moonlit night in the late twenties in the front quad of Wadham College seen from the porter's lodge. At the top right-hand corner of this pleasant, three-storeyed manor-house of a quadrangle, the work of Somerset masons, are the rooms of the dean. Raised and cheerful voices may be heard. Above them all, and louder, is the voice of Maurice, the Dean of Wadham, audible even from here. One did not have to look for Maurice, one only had to listen.

So lovable, loyal and formative a friend must be written about without a waste of words. Maurice despised journalism and pitied journalists. He was a stickler for grammar. There must be no hanging clauses, no verbless sentence in what I write about him here. He also despised television and refused to appear on it.

If one wants to hear an echo of Maurice's voice it may be heard sometimes in the conversation of Isaiah Berlin, Patrick Kinross and Osbert Lancaster – 'Couldn't agree with you more', 'Yers, yers – splendid!' But his resonant voice is needed and that 1914 army slang punctuated with 'old boy' and 'old man', to bring back the feeling of safe elation as the glass was thrust into one's hand and the introductions made to people one knew and liked already, but given different titles in the fantastic hierarchy Maurice invented for them.

And then there were his clothes. 'Why do you dress like an undergraduate, Betjeman?' he said to me some years after I had gone down. This was because I still wore a tweed coat and grey flannel trousers. Maurice himself was always in a suit, generally dark blue.

The Oxford of the late twenties, which was when I first came up, seemed to me to be divided, so far as undergraduates were concerned, between aesthetes and hearties. I was an aesthete. There would have been no hearties at the parties which I attended. Maurice's were always dinner parties. On the other hand we all

knew he was a great 'college man' and was held in high favour by
the rowing men of Wadham and he may have known Blues –
provided they came from Wadham. But he kept us all as sets, and
very much apart.

The guests I met at Maurice's dinner parties were generally
intellectuals, with a few young peers who may have been sons of
his friends of the 1914 war generation to which unexpectedly
Maurice belonged. We could not believe that anyone so free and
easy and unmilitary and scandalously entertaining could ever have
fought the Huns in trench warfare. He never mentioned it in the
twenties. We thought he was our own age.

I think his way of speaking with a strong emphasis on certain
syllables partly came from Winchester. Maurice, though a Chel-
tonian, was at New College, which was then an Oxford branch of
Winchester. I think it also came from Cambridge and such friends
there as Dadie Rylands and Adrian Bishop. It was a King's
Cambridge way of talking. Adrian Bishop was his closest and most
reckless friend in the twenties. Under the pleasure-lover, as with
Maurice, so with Adrian, there was the ascetic. Adrian, whose real
name was Frank, became an Anglican-Benedictine monk and took
the name of Brother Thomas More in religion. Maurice reconciled
himself to this change by referring to Adrian as 'Brother Tom'. I
still possess *A Sixteenth-Century Anthology* edited by Arthur
Symons which Adrian gave me with this inscription: 'To John
Betjeman, hoping that his thirty-first year may bring an increase in
tact, wisdom and courage. With love, from Frank Bishop.' The
censoriousness was characteristic of the stern self-discipline which
Maurice, Adrian and many of that generation imposed on themselves.

Because Wadham had an Evangelical tradition going back to
the time of Warden Symons who had arranged times of Chapel so
that undergraduates could not attend Newman's sermons in St
Mary's, Maurice also proclaimed himself an Evangelical. But his
Evangelicalism was only skin deep. One of his closest friends
among the Fellows of Wadham was Father Brabant, the Wadham
chaplain for many years, who was most distinctly Anglo-Catholic.
So were many of Maurice's friends. It was through one of these,
Lord Clonmore, that I first met Maurice. Pierse Synnott, an Irish
Roman-Catholic, was about the only Papist friend of Maurice in
these days. Maurice and I went to stay with both of these people

and I remember on one occasion Maurice coming into my bedroom when we were changing for dinner and saying, 'I say, old boy, shall we roger the skivvies?' The gift of exceeding the bounds of good taste was to me one of his endearing characteristics. There was a streak of Gowing in *The Diary of a Nobody* about Maurice which either attracted or repelled.

So outspoken a man contracted enemies. Sometimes it may have been simply a matter of genes. The rival host to undergraduates in the late twenties was the University Lecturer in Spanish, G. A. Kolkhorst, then known as 'G'ug' and later as 'Colonel' Kolkhorst because he was so little like a colonel. 'Charming fellow, Kolkhorst,' said Maurice. 'A pity he's got a touch of the tarbrush.' To which Colonel Kolkhorst, who was wholly white, replied by always referring to Maurice as 'Mr Borer'. It was a good early lesson in diplomacy to be acceptable to both Maurice and the Colonel, as neither of them stood any nonsense and exposed mockingly any pretension. Maurice, who was so alarming on first acquaintance with his machine-gun fire of quips and sudden slaying of popular idols, was kindness itself when one was in trouble. When I was rusticated he commiserated and had me to dinner, and even drove out with congenial friends to Thorpe House, Oval Way, Gerrards Cross, where I was working my passage as a private schoolmaster. He came to see my parents and induced them to continue an allowance to me and he secured for me, through his friendship with the owners of the Architectural Press, a position on the *Architectural Review* which enabled me to keep myself independent of my parents. What he did for me, who was not of his College, he did for all the Wadham undergraduates. He was their adviser and friend who gave practical help. During the last war he gave practical help to the victims of the Nazi Government and found them positions in England. Politically I should have said he was Left, but not doctrinaire. Hugh Gaitskell was a close friend, and many a wrangle over economics to which I did not listen did I hear at Maurice's table in my undergraduate days.

His most endearing quality was his power to build one up in one's own estimation. He did this by listening and either agreeing or suggesting a similar train of thought.

In the same way he took one's own troubles on his shoulders. Firmly and kindly he separated me from those he regarded as unsuitable. Cautiously and slowly he made friends of the opposite

sex who then became as close as his own generation had been. I
think particularly of Enid Starkie, Audrey Beecham, Dame Janet
Vaughan and my wife, to whom he was devoted, and Pam Hartwell,
Celli Clark and Anne Fleming. He forgave because he understood.
What he could not forgive was disloyalty and ruthlessness. He
was surprisingly kind and unshockable.

Maurice continued his kindness to the children of his friends.

But his greatest loves were Oxford as a place and Wadham
College as a society. He liked their buildings. My life is emptier
without those afternoons when he would ring up and say, 'What
about a look at Hertford and some Anglo-Jackson?' We would set
off in search of the many works in Oxford of the architect Sir
Thomas Jackson. Maurice would hear no word against him, for
Jackson had been a Fellow of Wadham.

His favourite colleges to visit when in architectural mood were
Hertford because of the Jackson work, Keble because of Butter-
field and his friend Crab Owen, and Pembroke because he admired
the members of its Common Room and Dr Homes-Dudden, its
Master.

In the twenties and thirties Maurice would venture further
afield in hired cars driven very fast and dangerously by undergraduates. He did not drive himself. He took us to Garsington
and Lady Ottoline and Sezincote, and of course we went out very
fast to dine at the Spread Eagle at Thame at Fothergill's.

Once, when the car I was driving waltzed around in the road
near Moreton-in-Marsh and buckled its wheels, he was quite
unmoved. But I remember once taking him to see the inside of the
Cowley Fathers' Mission House in Manston Street. That was the
only time I knew him alarmed.

In later life he liked walking in North Oxford, especially in
places like Belbroughton Road where he would look at houses in
which he might retire. Another favourite walk was Holywell
Cemetery, where he looked at the headstones to great brains and
Heads of Houses now dust in erstwhile meadowland. He is buried
there himself.

Shall any of us who knew him enjoy life so much as we did in
his company? I can hear him say 'Definitely *no*'.

8

Anthony Powell

The Bowra World and Bowra Lore

During my first year at Oxford (I went up in October, 1923) I often heard the name of Maurice Bowra spoken, but without gaining much idea of what this rather famous young don was like, nor why he was famous. We did not meet, I think, until my third term, the summer, when one afternoon Pierse (in those days more usually 'Piers') Synott, also at Balliol (denounced by A. D. Lindsay, when Master, as a 'gilded popinjay', but later *haut fonctionnaire* of the Admiralty), brought Bowra, then Dean of Wadham, round to my rooms in college.

Noticeably small, this lack of stature emphasised by a massive head and tiny feet, Bowra – especially in later life – looked a little like those toys which cannot be pushed over because heavily weighted at the base; or perhaps Humpty-Dumpty, whose autocratic diction and quick-fire interrogations were also paralleled. As against that, the short ringing laughs likely to accompany Bowra's comments were not at all characteristic of Humpty-Dumpty's rather sour resentment, though their tenor could be equally ominous.

Bowra possessed a considerable presence. As a don, he habitually wore a hat and a suit, the last, during festive periods like Commem, sometimes varied by flannel trousers, light grey, though never outrageously 'Oxford' in cut. The suits were in different shades of brown, very neat, always tending to look a shade tight over the outline of a figure essentially solid rather than plump. One used 'Maurice' as form of address, but a note from him (usually an invitation) would always be signed 'CMB'.

This social call went off pretty well. Conversation turning for some reason on Byron (rather a favourite topic of Bowra's as it happened), he remarked that, in his hearing at the Gilbert Murrays' recently, a visiting notability had asked: 'Are you interested in incest, Professor Murray?', to which the Regius Professor of Greek had gently answered: 'In a general way.'

After the Balliol meeting I was to some extent included in the Bowra *monde* – or rather one of them, for there were not a few – an affiliation which perceptibly developed the following year, when Henry Yorke (Henry Green, the novelist), whom I had known since preparatory school days, and at Eton, came up to Magdalen. Yorke, through connexions of his own, almost immediately registered as a Bowra friend. Together we used to see a fair amount of Bowra, especially when we both inhabited undergraduate rooms on the top floor of 4 King Edward Street (lodgings in a robust music-hall tradition, kept by the redoubtable Mrs Collins), where Yorke and I would almost obsessively mull over the Bowra world and Bowra lore. It was a world which partook of various others in Oxford – avoiding the extreme position of either 'Aesthete' or 'Hearty' – although in itself always a little apart from any of the other worlds of which it might partake.

Immensely generous, Bowra entertained a great deal at Wadham; in my own experience, always undergraduates. I can never recall meeting a don in his rooms, though no doubt that was simply a matter of segregation. The dinner-parties were of six or eight, good college food, lots to drink, almost invariably champagne, much laughter and gossip, always a slight sense of danger. This faint awareness of apprehension was by no means imaginary, because the host could easily take offence (usually without visible sign, except to an expert) at an indiscreet word striking a wrong, anyway personally unpleasing note, in dialogues which were, nevertheless, deliberately aimed at indiscretion. Bowra's reaction was likely to be announced a day or two later.

'What so-and-so said the other night has just come back as Bad Blood.'

The rooms themselves were simply furnished, with few pictures; what pictures, I do not remember. Later, at the Warden's house, there was a drawing of Bowra himself by Henry Lamb, which dated, I think, from a visit to Pakenham (now Tullynally) in the early thirties, when he and the Lambs had been staying in the house at the same time. The larger surfaces to be regulated in the Warden's house underlined this taste for austere interior decoration, a characteristic worth mention as reflecting Bowra's energetic, practical nature, concerned with action, rather than amelioration of his own surroundings; an aspect of himself in contrast with

his other – if you like, 'poetic' – side, and one he would perhaps
have preferred more evenly balanced.

The impact on myself, as an undergraduate, of Bowra's personality and wit is not easy to define, so various were its workings. If
the repeated minor shock from this volcano took many forms,
their earliest, most essential, was a sense of release. Here was a don
– someone by his very calling, anyway to some extent, suspect as
representative (in those days) of authority and discipline, an official
promoter of didacticism – who so far from directly or indirectly
attempting to expound tedious moral values of an old-fashioned
kind, openly praised the worship of Pleasure.

Of course those of us who had got as far as the Nineties at
school – that is to say anybody, one felt, who had any claim to
consideration – were already familiar with 'older people' who
recommended a romantic Wildean paganism, but Bowra went
further, much further, than that. He was also totally free from a, by
then, rather musty (though at Oxford by no means defunct)
Nineties aestheticism. Everything about him was up-to-date. The
innovation was not only to proclaim the paramount claims of eating,
drinking and sex (if necessary, auto-erotic), but accepting as absolutely natural open snobbishness, success worship, personal vendet-
tas, unprovoked malice, disloyalty to friends, reading other people's
letters (if not lying about, to be sought in unlocked drawers) –
the whole bag of tricks of what most people think and feel and
often act on, yet are themselves ashamed of admitting they do and
feel and think.

In connexion with personal hates – Bowra made no bones about
these – was his suggestion of the Bête Noire Club. Subscribing
members of the Club were each allowed one name to put on its
list, to be circulated to all members, who, irrespective of whether
or not they personally had anything against the individual concerned, would secretly persecute him on every possible occasion.
Not only was the Bowra gospel sustained with excellent jokes, it
was seasoned with a sound commonsense and down-to-earthness,
distinguishing it not only from pretentious high-thinking, but also
from brutal pursuit of self-interest divorced from good manners.

'You don't get the best value out of your selfishness, if you're
selfish all the time.'

Perhaps some analogy might be drawn between first coming into
contact with Bowra, and an initiatory dip into the works of

Nietzsche; although, so far as I know, Nietzsche's altar was not one where Bowra burned much, if any, incense. No modern philosopher, but the Ancient Greeks, supplied all he loved and stood for. That, at least, was the impression he chose to give.

The Bowra delivery, loud, stylised, ironic, usually followed by those deep abrupt bursts of laughter, was superlatively effective in attack. I have heard it suggested that another alumnus of Bowra's school (Cheltenham), one a few years older than himself, was reputed to possess a somewhat similar detonative form of speech – thereby suggesting a common Cheltenhamian source, probably a master there – but no details were available, and this rumour has never, so far as is known, been authenticated. It is rather the sort of thing people invent. Even if a foundation had already been laid, Bowra himself had undoubtedly perfected the mechanism, formidable, succinct, ear-splitting, in a manner that could only be regarded as his own. Its echoes are to be heard to this day in the tones of disciples, who, in an unfledged state, came heavily under Bowra influence.

One felt immediately on meeting him for the first time that Bowra was a man quite different from any met before. This was certainly true of myself; also, I think, of most other undergraduates, whether they liked him or not. Some very definitely did not. He was prepared – for an acutely sensitive man, as he himself always proclaimed, far too prepared – to make enemies. To any questions about drawbacks in his own nature from which he had suffered, he had an invariable reply.

'A skin too few. Yet one continues to go out of one's way to court people's hatred.'

I am, of course, speaking of the young Bowra. As in the Beerbohm series of Old and Young selves, there was modification – though not all that much modification – with increased age and fame. No doubt sides had always been hidden away from what was revealed to undergraduates, who were simply admitted to an astonishing vision of forbidden things accepted as a matter of course, and with appropriate laughter. K. N. Bell, my history tutor at Balliol, used to say: 'The wall round the Senior Common Room is a low one, but there is a wall'. Bowra, most of the time, ignored this comparatively artificial barrier. I remember the unexpectedness of a sudden reminder of his own professional status, sense of what was academically correct, when, after a noisy dinner-party at Wadham, someone (not myself) wandering round Bowra's sitting-room, suddenly asked: 'Why, Maurice, what are these?'

Bowra jumped up as if dynamited.

'Put those down at once. They're Schools papers. No, indeed . . .'

A moment later he was locking away in a drawer the candidates' answers to their examination, laughing, but, for a second, he had been angry. The astonishment I felt at the time in this (very justifiable) call to order shows how skilfully Bowra normally handled his parties of young men. At the same time, even in those early days, it was from time to time apparent that Bowra himself was not immune from falling victim to Bowra doctrine, a fact that he – anyway in later life – was far too intelligent not to recognise, and ironically to acknowledge. The showmanship was usually brilliant, never in the least fraudulent, but only the more naive of spectators could fail to grasp that a proportion of it was purely defensive. There were less well fortified Bowra positions, as well as the well fortified ones. The former sometimes proved vulnerable, not so much to deliberate assault, as to undesigned incursions on the part of disciples speaking too frankly; indeed speaking in the manner Bowra himself had taught them. They would, for instance, report back painful things other people had said about Bowra himself, which, very naturally, he did not always appreciate. Nevertheless, he would stick to his guns, and usually came out on top, or not far from that.

Certain matters, unclear at the time, fall into better perspective when one looks back; notably the 'age-gap' of the twenties, a chasm making all subsequent ones of its sort seem inconsiderable. Men and women grown up before 1914 were not only older, they were altogether set apart from my generation. Thus they remained throughout life; you never caught up with them. This was true, broadly speaking, whether or not they had been actively involved in hostilities, but it was particularly true (though, paradoxically, within this category, sometimes superficially obscured) of the younger men, like Bowra, those nearer in age to my own lot. These war veterans of no great age had, on the one hand, known a world already disappeared; on the other, were keenly conscious (their juniors too, but they only feeling their way) of new, still undefined forms of existence, which, come what may, they were determined to explore and exploit.

My own Oxford generation (by now not unjustly typed as a

decidedly ambitious crew) was the first of that decade to live in a university untinged by the ex-soldier and his ways. People who had been 'in the war' might seem a million to us, yet only the previous year there had been undergraduates in residence liable to speak of 'hall' as 'mess', and otherwise indulge in obsolete, barely decent locutions deriving from military life. Such jargon was naturally deplored by the more sophisticated ex-campaigners, but even these latter were inexpungibly branded by age and war-service in the eyes of the oncoming waves of aspiring schoolboys.

Bowra, less than eight years older than myself, must have been just twenty-six when I first knew him. That fact now seems altogether beyond belief. Certainly, as I have indicated, he navigated with perfect ease the waters dividing undergraduate and don. Beyond that stream was a flood not to be crossed, an intangible sense of experience, which then – and for ever – set those who had been 'in the war' apart. Belonging to this strange, fascinating brood of survivors, Bowra had come up to New College not only older than the average pre-war or post-war freshman (and far more intelligent), but, with others of his species, already on familiar terms with sex and death. He often spoke of the former; very rarely of the latter.

At that period he did not often speak of the war at all, then always with mimicry and laughter. ('Got a boil on your cock, old boy, then crash along to the M.O., who'll soon put you right with a Number 9'; or his own battery-commander's commendation of *Artillery Training*: 'A book written by far cleverer men than me or you'). All the same, I am inclined to think that the comparatively short (though not unadventurous) time Bowra spent in the army played a profound part in his thoughts and inner life. I think it possible that even at those Wadham dinner-parties, when the uproar was at its height, not least on the part of the host, the days and friends of the war were never far from Bowra's mind.

Not long after he came up, Henry Yorke penetrated Lady Ottoline Morrell's 'circle' at Garsington, to which in due course he introduced me also. Bowra was already an habitué, but even he was prepared to recognise that a Garsington invitation was not something to be treated lightly. For the most experienced in salon life, Garsington represented moving up into the firing-line; for a nervous undergraduate, an ordeal of the most gruelling order.

Garsington conditions have often been described, emphasis

usually laid on the exotic appearance and behaviour of the hostess, both of which certainly had to be reckoned with. The worst perplexities always seemed to me to lie rather in an utter uncertainty as to what level of life there ought to be assumed by the guest. A sense of 'pre-war' constraint – or what one imagined that to be – always prevailed. There was also likely to be present one more or less wild man; a bohemian exhibit, making appropriately naive bohemian remarks. To have these addressed to oneself, especially during one of the many silences that fell, was something to be dreaded. Alternatively, you might be caught out in quite a different manner, by forgetting, say, the date of Ascot, or the name of some nobleman's 'place'. On the whole the legend of imposing intellectual conversation was the least of the threats. The arts, if discussed at all, were approached in a manner that – if such can be said without offence – might reasonably be called middlebrow; though no less alarming for that. It was like acting in a play – or rather several quite different plays somehow fused together – in which you had not been told either the plot or your own cue; sometimes a drawing-room comedy; sometimes an Expressionist curtain-raiser; sometimes signs loomed up of an old-fashioned Lyceum melodrama.

This last stage effect had been involuntarily brought into being by Bowra – a great retailer of Garsington stories – when staying in the house, in itself something of a distinction. Coming down to breakfast early, he had inadvertently eaten the toast (possibly Ryvita, even if toast, toast of some special sort) found in the toast-rack. A short time later Lady Ottoline arrived. She looked round the table. Something was wrong. She rang the bell.

'*Where is my toast?*'

Lady Ottoline's very individual manner of speaking, a kind of cooing nasal hiss – often imitated, but never in the least successfully – was at its most threatening.

The parlour-maid, herself well known as a formidable character, fixed her eyes on Bowra.

'The toast was there when *he* came down, m'lady . . .'

Bowra, Yorke and I were on our way to luncheon at Garsington once, when, I remember, Bowra remarked that he had had his hair cut – 'makes one more presentable'. The word 'presentable', not particularly notable in that context, was a very important epithet in the Bowra system of social terminology; a system which had to be picked up and adhered to by the neophyte. That was not at all difficult on account of its convenient terseness, and the manner in which it had been designed to cover most human types at Oxford, and elsewhere. Indeed, its total adoption was hard to resist, and one of the forms of power that Bowra exercised over his disciples.

'Presentable' was not merely an important label, but a *sine qua non* for acceptance into the Bowra scheme of things. There were certainly Bowra acquaintances, kept in the background, who never quite succeeded in qualifying, yet (Bowra being kindhearted as well as ruthless) were still allowed some access. The limbo they occupied did not go so far as the very damaging absolute antithesis 'unpresentable'. Those who had 'unpresentable' pinned on them were remorselessly barred.

'Able' (or 'able, I'm afraid') probably did not signify personal approval, but was, at worst, a fairly high commendation. 'Upright', also not lightly accorded, might be held in its way equally complimentary (if you cared about old-fashioned honourable dealings), but was likely to carry overtones a shade satirical, with also no guarantee of friendliness. 'Nice stupid man', hardly flattering to the object of its designation, was at the same time well disposed, and accorded relatively sparingly. 'Shit of hell', a status in the severest degree derogatory, in practice inclined to imply, as well as hearty dislike, an element of uneasy suspicion, sometimes amounting to acknowledged fear.

Bowra made great play with these categories, which were an established part of his verbal barrage. There were other important phrases, such as 'make bad blood' (referred to earlier) and 'cause pain'. 'Bad blood' might be used in two rather different senses. Bowra would say: 'I made splendid bad blood between so-and-so and so-and-so over such-and-such a matter', laughing a lot at the thought of what he had brought about; he would also, as has been said, speak gloomily of 'bad blood' made in relation to himself. This latter might be deliberate vilification, or an accidental remark later conceived as having snide bearing on himself. 'Cause pain' was likely to refer not to specific attacks of his own or other people, but the success or good luck of individuals which brought pangs of envy or jealousy on hearing the news. 'Cause pain' may have had its origin in the hero of R. L. Stevenson's *The Wrong Box*, who used to say: 'Anything to cause a little pain.'

These Bowra approaches to life, jocular yet practical, provoking both laughter and trepidation, are hard to preserve on paper. That

G

is true of his – and all other – wit. Bowra's could be of the carefully perfected order (none the worse for that), set-pieces produced with a flourish on social occasions, many examples of which remain on record. Good talkers are apt to be remembered for these comparatively elaborate *mots*. Excellent as these could be in their own field, Bowra's throwaway allusions and comebacks often surpassed them, thereby marking him out (which cannot be said of all good talkers) as a wit who neither required previous prepartion for what he said, nor saved up all the good stuff for smart company. The ephemeral nature of such good remarks prevented them from passing into history, since they ornamented conversations too trivial to remember or reconstruct; for example, someone (perhaps myself) commented on a story just told: 'On earth the broken wind . . .'; to which Bowra without pause added: '. . . in the heaven, a perfect sound.'

The Bowra world was one where there must be no uncertainty. A clearcut decision had to be made about everything and everybody – good, bad – desirable, undesirable – nice man, shit of hell. This method naturally included intellectual judgments, and taste in works of art. In one sense, nothing is more to be aimed at in approaching such matters than lucid, uncompromising thought; in another, the arts are always an area of uncertainty in their creation, a good deal of latitude being allowed for experiment. In the Bowra world there was little or no concession to uncertainty – latterly that was perhaps less true – and, when I first knew Bowra, he himself always suggested a sense of uneasiness at activities in that line of too independent a sort. That was, of course, within the sphere of Bowra himself being, in principle, always well-disposed to what was 'advanced'. Bowra himself, with all his intelligence and spoken wit, remained throughout life inexplicably unhandy at writing. He was a capable, if academic and rather uninspiring literary critic. His comic poems were comic, no more. They possessed no unique quality. Any field in which he did not excel was a distress to him, the literary one most of all; therefore I think – for young men who wanted to develop along lines of their own – it was best to know Bowra, then get away; if necessary return to him in due course to appreciate the many things he had to offer.

An incident one now sees as walking a social tight-rope, but at the time seemed an amusing intellectual experiment, was a dinner-party Yorke and I gave at King Edward Street, to which, among others, we asked Bowra and my Balliol tutor, Kenneth Bell. This dinner appeared a great success at the time, even though Bowra had commented without enthusiasm on hearing Bell was to be one of the guests. Throughout the evening, Bell, in his own hearty, erratic manner a man of great charm and brilliance, let fly a fusillade of fireworks; Bowra keeping relatively quiet. One grasps now that such a dinner-table combination was not a very tactful one, both from general principles of the unwisdom of mixing too strong personalities – over-seasoning in cooking – and, in this particular case, playing tricks with Bowra's own very delicate relationship with the dons of that day; some of whom were inclined to raise an eyebrow at the ease with which he moved among undergraduates. Bell moved easily among undergraduates too, but in a very different manner. In fact, the two of them belonged to such diversified categories of don that no great harm was done, but the risk had been great.

I can now see that dinner-party as giving opportunity to learn, which I did not take. Had I been quicker to comprehend its intricacies, later events might have been less gauchely handled; although, as things fell out, that – so far as I myself was concerned – could have been for the best.

A year or more after I first met Bowra, I was spending the vacation in rather depressing circumstances living with my parents in a 'private hotel' on the outskirts of Andover in Hampshire. After a spell on the staff, my father had returned to regimental duty with his battalion, stationed in that area. We had been unable to find a house near Tidworth (or wherever it was), and were camped out, more or less indefinitely, in this dismal spot. One afternoon – I cannot remember the time of year, but summer rather than winter – an obviously hired car turned into the short drive, and stopped at the door of the hotel.

Out of the car stepped Bowra, and again, as it happened, Synnott, who had perhaps been driving, though some memory remains of a chauffeur. Certainly Bowra was not at the wheel. It appeared, so far as I can remember, that Synnott had been staying up for some weeks of vac (probably in order to work for Greats), and, he and Bowra coming over to this part of the country for a jaunt (perhaps to visit the sights of Winchester), had decided to pay a call – though I cannot imagine how they knew where I was living. This was unprecedented excitement in the bleak Andover day.

They stayed for tea. When it was time to return to Oxford, Bowra put forward the suggestion, which may even have been represented as the object of the visit, that I should come back with them: Bowra would put me up for a day or two at Wadham. It would make a change. Synnott, I feel pretty sure, was almost immediately on his way home.

I accepted this proposal in the manner one accepted so much at that age, just as something that happened. It was all rather an adventure. I was very glad to get away from Andover, even for a short time. I did not give much thought to what might be expected of me at the receiving end – which was, I suppose, to make myself reasonably agreeable for a few days, then return home without overstaying my welcome. I remained in Oxford for two or three days, then came back to Andover, but, entirely owing to my own fault, the visit was not a success. This was due to a lack of discernment that goes with immaturity. There was also little to do in Oxford out of term (Bowra himself naturally occupied with his own academic activities during most of the day), and I was scarcely less bored pacing the High than back at the Andover hotel.

One evening, dining tête-à-tête with Bowra in his rooms, I spoke of how little I liked being at Oxford, and how I longed to get it over and go down. The lack of finesse in voicing such sentiments in the particular circumstances was, of course, altogether inexcusable. The idea that Bowra himself was a young man with a career still ahead of him, about which he no doubt suffered still all sorts of uncertainties, even horrors, never crossed my mind. He seemed a grown-up person for whom all was settled. In a sense, from one point of view, that made my gaffe even worse. My own sentiments were unusual for an undergraduate of that generation, most of whom (Yorke another exception) regarded – still regard – their Oxford days as the happiest, etc. etc. One learns in due course (without always achieving the aim in practice) that, more often than not, it is better to keep deeply felt views about oneself to oneself. In any case a little good sense – a little good manners even – might have warned me that a confession of just that sort was not one to make to a slightly older friend, who, even then, was becoming one of the ever-brightening fixed stars of the Oxford firmament. Bowra hospitality had no doubt played a part in inducing such plain speaking, but I make no attempt to put that forward in extenuation.

In short, it took some thirty-five years for our relations to recover from that evening in Wadham. I was not put in anything like the worst disgrace possible, condemned to the unmitigated outer darkness offenders might be liable to, especially those about whom the phrase 'treading on people's corns' had been used – and not at the time understood. Indeed, beyond the adoption of a somewhat tarter form of address, and a falling off of invitations, no spectacular censure took place. We continued to meet while I remained up at Oxford, later sometimes running across each other in London.

Although I regret my maladroitness in causing this rift, I am not sure – as suggested above – whether for my own good it was not just as well to be withdrawn from Bowra influence, before the grip became all but irremovable. Probably disjunction would in any case have taken place; seeds of disagreement existing at the stage each of us was approaching, a break inevitable.

When I was briefly attached to Intelligence Corps Headquarters at Oxford during the war, Bowra lunched with my wife and me at the Randolph. All went well, even if things were not quite on the footing they once had been. Professor Lindemann had just been raised to the peerage as Lord Cherwell.

'Don't mind that. Don't mind at all,' Bowra said. 'Causes pain. You wouldn't believe the pain it's caused.'

I emphasise this change of relation, not because of great interest in itself – it could hardly be of less – but on account of the manner in which it divided my acquaintance with Bowra into two quite separate periods: the first, Bowra in his late twenties; the second, Bowra in his early sixties: the sort of pattern that appeals to the instincts of a professional writer.

A year or two after the war I met, quite by chance, when we had taken a holiday cottage in the country, a young man who turned out to be an undergraduate at Wadham, of which Bowra was by then Warden. I asked how he got on with the head of the house. The young man did not stint his praise. He could hardly sufficiently commend a man of such distinction, for whom no member of the college was too humble to be noticed, none too geographically remote to be kept in touch with on going down; understanding, amusing, hard working, the Warden was a don in a million.

'But,' added the young Wadhamite, 'I've heard he's an absolute fish out of water, when he's away from the academic world he's accustomed to.'

I really cannot imagine any typification which would have annoyed Bowra more; nor one that was less true. The words are, however, of interest: first, by illustrating how easy it is to make misjudgments at an early age (not necessarily only then); secondly, by showing how heartily Bowra threw himself into the Warden's role. To the inexperienced it seemed impossible that he could possess any other interest. This capacity for taking on with enthusiasm forms of life alien to those with which he was commonly associated – in short, the exact opposite to what the undergraduate supposed – was well illustrated by Bowra on Hellenic cruises.

Never to have seen Bowra on an Hellenic cruise was to have missed an essential aspect of him. The ship would contain close on three hundred passengers, of whom more than half might come from the United States. Bowra would from time to time lecture, and in general propagate, sometimes in an indirect manner too, the archaeological sites to be visited. His lectures at Oxford were not, anyway in the eyes of his colleagues, regarded as his forte, but the ones he gave on these cruises were another matter. No one who heard him in the museum at Olympia (Centaurs and Lapiths) could be anything but richly stimulated; an experience really worth having. It might be supposed that someone by this time famous as a scholar and personality might have become a trifle unapproachable by the run-of-the-mill tourist. Nothing could have been further from that, nor from his former pupil's assessment of Bowra removed from the academic setting; at least this was a very different kind of academic setting. Bowra was just as likely to be seen at a table of delighted grey-haired matrons from West Kensington or the Middle West, as exchanging cracks with Mortimer Wheeler (or what might snobbishly be regarded as tourist élite) over a *raki* at the bar.

In 1960, my wife and I went on one of these Hellenic cruises, which included putting in at Sardinia, Sicily, Malta, North Africa, as well as Greece. When, with the rest of the party, we met at London Airport, there was a second when one wondered how things were going to go, so far as the Bowra relationship was concerned. The plane flew to Milan, then there was a longish bus journey to Genoa. Bowra and I sat next to each other on the bus. We talked a lot. Old contacts were re-established. The détente was complete.

At Malta, Bowra asked us (with our fourteen-year-old younger son) to dine with him at a restaurant he knew on the island. This restaurant was situated on the higher levels of Valetta. We reached it on the way out by taxi; Bowra explaining that we could more easily return by public lift, which, operating at regular intervals, grounded its passengers only a short way from the harbour, and our ship.

We dined enjoyably, and strolled to the place of the lift. A notice on it indicated that we had missed the last descent by ten minutes, and were faced with a long and steep descent on foot.

Four-letter words have been rather overdone of late years, but, when the ex-Vice-Chancellor of Oxford University, President of the British Academy, holder of innumerable honorific degrees and international laurels, expressed himself (and the feelings of the rest of us) it was intensely funny.

'Fuck!'

The monosyllable must have carried as far as the African coast.

We were on a second cruise with Bowra when the ship passed through the Dardanelles. As we sailed by the shore of Gallipoli, in a brief, quite unemphasised ceremony, a wreath was committed to the sea. Some days later I remarked to Bowra that, although the best part of fifty years had passed, the moment of the wreath's descent to the waves had been moving, even rather upsetting. I was not quite prepared for the violence of agreement.

'Had to go below. Lie down for *half-an-hour* afterwards in my cabin.'

After this second cruise with Bowra, he asked me to be his guest at the 'Dorothy' dinner, and we stayed at Wadham. On the morning we left I was with him in the hall of the Warden's House, when an undergraduate (wearing a beard) arrived to ask a question or obtain some permission. Bowra fired out questions in the old accustomed explosive manner. The young man did not react. One knew that an amused – even a naive – reflex would immediately achieve a favourable result, but no reaction at all was visible. The undergraduate went away.

'I don't understand them at all nowadays,' Bowra said.

Later in the year Bowra came to us for a weekend. It was during this visit that something (in addition to Gallipoli) convinced me of how much the 'first' war had meant to him. We took him to dine with some neighbours. There was certainly plenty to drink, but that did not altogether explain what followed after dinner. Bowra insisted – he really did insist – on the whole party spending the rest of the evening singing 'There's a long, long trail a-winding and 'Pack up your troubles in your old kitbag'. Perhaps by then he did not often find himself in company where such behaviour was even conceivable. I suppose it is just possible that an evening might have ended in the same way in the days when I had first known him, but I never remember anything of the sort, and in any case it would then have been somehow different.

Two additional cruise incidents should go on record. My wife had just been dancing the *Blue Danube* waltz with Bowra. This was the sole dance he recognised, first of all (she reported) pawing the ground like a little bull entering the ring. When we were sitting together afterwards, speaking of invitations, domestic arrangements – some trivial matter, its subject forgotten – she let fall a quite thoughtless comment:

'But surely that's easy enough for a carefree bachelor like you, Maurice.'

Bowra was suddenly discomposed.

'Never, *never*, use that term of me again.'

He laughed immediately after, but for a moment it had been no laughing matter; perhaps a sudden touch of what he himself, in the old days, had called 'creeping bitterness'.

The other matter arose one afternoon sailing past Samothrace. Kipling's name had cropped up. Bowra said: 'Have you ever played the game of marking yourself for the qualities listed in *If*—? It's a good one.'

We set about playing the game at once. Rather unexpectedly, Bowra knew the poem by heart. I now greatly regret that I did not immediately afterwards write down the attributes Bowra claimed (he was very modest about them), and also the correct system of marking. My impression is that you could clock up half a mark for possessing the characteristic in principle, another half for improving on the situation; that is to say trusting yourself when all men doubt you, scoring additionally for making allowance for their doubting too. It is, however, possible that you were assessed for five, out of each combined condition. The second system is less likely, because I seem to recall that Bowra gave himself a total of only three-and-a-half out of a potential fifteen, or thereabouts. His comments greatly augmented the pleasures of the game.

'Being lied about, don't deal in lies – that's absurd, of course. Next one.'

We came to Triumph and Disaster.

'Can't say about Triumph. Never experienced it.'

'Maurice, what nonsense.'

But he was adamant. He had never known Triumph. All the same, he had liked playing the *If—* game, and was in very good form after it.

9

Osbert Lancaster

A Very Salutary Experience

One depressing winter's day in the middle of the Second World War I left the Ministry of Information to go for a walk with Isaiah Berlin. The object of our stroll was that Isaiah, over on a flying visit from Washington, should 'put me in the picture', as the current jargon had it, regarding the then state of American public opinion. However, we had got no farther than Woburn Square when the informative stream suddenly dried up and my companion pointed, in astonished and uncharacteristic silence, to a small, resolute figure rapidly approaching from the other end of the street. Was it, could it be, the Warden of Wadham? It was. What on earth, we asked ourselves, was Maurice doing, wandering round Bloomsbury on this chilly wartime afternoon? Was he *en route* for the Ministry in pursuance of some elaborate intrigue to topple Prof. Lindemann? Did he, perhaps, maintain a secret love-nest tucked away in Gordon Square? Fascinating as were the speculations to which his presence gave rise, an even greater interest was likely to attach, as Isaiah at once pointed out, to the explanation offered. We did not have long to wait; hardly had we come within earshot, which, given Maurice's conversational range, was a little over a hundred yards, when we had our as yet unsolicited reward. 'I have just been visiting the church where Christina Rossetti used to worship. Very moving!'

Once more the Warden had triumphantly demonstrated his extraordinary ability never to be caught out. No matter how unexpected or potentially embarrassing the question, no one ever knew him to be at a loss for an immediate, or even, as in this case, preemptive reply; not always relevant, but invariably conclusive.

Nowhere was this exceptional alertness more effective than on the croquet lawn. This agreeable pastime, of which the Warden was extremely fond, is governed, I believe, by an elaborate, and doubtless clearly defined, set of rules, but one of which, in my experience, the interpretation usually varies in accordance with the number of players involved. But not at Wadham. Maurice, for whom in any game speed was of the essence, would brook no delay, and any difference of opinion was always immediately and authoritatively resolved in ringing tones which defied all contradiction. The law thus firmly established, he would sweep impetuously on from hoop to hoop, as regardless of murmured protests as he was of casualties, which were not infrequent, for with Maurice behind the ball only billiard fives carried a higher risk of physical injury.

This determination to have everything cut and dried, to leave no room for time-wasting, and possibly mischievous, speculation, even if it did not in every case achieve its object, was, I think, closely allied to his formidable tidiness. Every time one entered that small, ground-floor room, in the Warden's Lodgings, where he was accustomed to receive visitors, one's spirits sank afresh. No trace of personality did it reveal; the furniture was as severely arranged as in a provincial French salon or a Harley Street waiting-room; no cigarette-ends sullied the ash-trays, and the blank expanse of the table-top was unrelieved by any scrap of paper or empty glass or casually laid aside book. The curtains and chair-covers were provocatively undemonstrative, and the few pictures on the walls were tributes to his friendship with the artists responsible rather than the outcome of any process of aesthetic selection. Everything was protectively neutral. And then the door would be flung open and the whole atmosphere was at once changed and recharged.

So great was the warmth and excitement which the Warden's presence immediately generated that the bleakness of the setting seemed not just irrelevant but justified. Any more elaborate décor, hinting at personal taste or revelatory of character – such as the Japanese knick-knacks and Beardsley drawings which provided the necessary act-drop for the Sage of Beaumont Street – could only, one now realised, have proved distracting. Like Verdi's *Falstaff*, Maurice was a grand opera that needed no overture.

As soon as the curtain rose the first great recitative began. That Maurice was a dominating conversationalist was undeniable, but he was handicapped by his personality for, although unquestionably the greatest raconteur of his time, so stimulating was his personality that he invariably excited all present to emulation. In his company the dullest economist or the beefiest peer in the Bullingdon was wont uncharacteristically to sparkle, and the resulting volume of sound filled not only the room but the whole quad. And then suddenly silence fell; Maurice had decided the time had come for paper-games.

In Wadham paper-games were taken seriously; none of the uncertainties or delays which render such pastimes so tedious, when played in country houses, was tolerated for a moment. The subjects were set by the host – a brief biography of the President of Magdalen in heroic couplets, or 'Consequences' in the metre of Locksley Hall – as was the pace, which permitted of no dawdling. Brilliant as were the results – not unexpectedly, as the players were hand-picked – Maurice's own contributions were invariably the most memorable, thanks largely to his awareness of exactly how far he could go and his habit of then going a great deal further.

If the company was small and intimate these great ensembles would be followed, after a short interval for more champagne, by a series of solo arias. Having taken down from its locked shelf the famous manuscript volume, on which no eye but the poet's had ever been allowed to rest, he would settle himself in his chair, raise a hand for silence and begin the reading.

First would come a selection of the old favourites – 'The Ballad of Bob Boothby' in the manner of Thomas Hardy, perhaps, or the 'Ode to Penelope Betjeman' – and then, if we were lucky, would follow the première of a new and recently completed composition. This would be rendered in deeper and even more impressive tones, the subtleties and more lyrical passages emphasised by monitory finger-wagging or free and sweeping gestures of the hand. At the end he would turn interrogatively to the company, 'Rather beautiful don't you think?' We did, and very privileged we felt to have been present, for at such recitals the audience was strictly limited. Only once do I recall his giving a public performance. One night during the blitz, carried away by port, enthusiasm and the prospect of an air-raid, which he always found particularly stimulating, he recited the whole of the Epithalamion for Kenneth Clark in the middle of Pratt's Club to an audience consisting of Evelyn Waugh, Lord Birkenhead, a handful of puzzled but attentive ensigns from the Brigade of Guards, and myself.

Curiously enough the fruits of his great learning were seldom garnished with humour, and in his published works and his lectures (but not, I believe, in his tutorials) that ebullience which characterised his social life was carefully muted. It was as though he feared that his eminence as a scholar might be compromised by his celebrity as a wit. Maybe he was right, but nevertheless it was, I think, in the latter role that his influence was greater and more beneficent. If ever that overworked adjective 'life-enhancing', so dear to Berenson, could be properly applied, it was to Maurice. And fortunate indeed were those of us who in youth experienced it. Any occasion was enriched by his presence: bathing in the Starnberger See with Maurice swimming round very high out of the water (his mastery of the breast-stroke was peculiarly his own) reciting Rilke at the top of his voice; visiting some Oxford church with Maurice leaping into the pulpit to give an imitation of Dr Dudden or some other eminent University preacher; singing 'Sumer is icumen in' at the village concert with that roof-raising baritone invariably coming in half a bar too soon. Such experiences were formative, demonstrating as they did that opportunities for enjoy-ment were to be grasped wherever found, simultaneously if need be, and need not await categorisation as intellectual, physical or aes-thetic; that limits existed to be exceeded, provided the feat was accomplished spontaneously, with style and without self-con-sciousness. No man was ever less moved by a vulgar desire to *épater les bourgeois*, and none was quicker to detect, and deal with, those who were. The wind blew where it listed, usually at gale force, but was always (or almost always) tempered to the shorn lamb; the privileges of age were duly acknowledged and genuine convictions firmly held and, if need be, logically defended, were respected. But pomposity, *amour-propre* and self-satisfaction went down like ninepins and for a generation still slightly overawed by established reputations and unquestioned eminence a very salu-tary experience it was.

10

John H. Finley Jr

Maurice in America: I

Maurice was first at Harvard in the autumn term of 1936, in the year after Milman Parry's death and during the later sway of E. K. Rand, Stanley Pease and the granitic but admired teacher C. N. Jackson, the monarch of the Department. He had known Felix Frankfurter, then still at the Law School, and the literary scholar J. L. Lowes in their Oxford years as Eastman Professors, but other doors quickly opened to him and, as he describes in his *Memories*, he gained astonishing width of acquaintance. I was a young instructor settling down after years abroad. American Hellenists less easily find companionship in the subject than do their British and European counterparts, and Parry's loss was heavy. It is impossible to convey my vernal joy and sense of fortune in Maurice. He was a little older than I; with *Tradition and Design in the Iliad* not long behind him, was in the first flight of his huge verve and talent; overflowed with allusion to people who had meant most to him, notably Murray, Wade-Gery, and Denniston; though in full days, he seemed endlessly free to talk about Greek. I still hear his booming voice behind passages that we read. By later accounts and in letters from Harvardians at Oxford, especially from the line of people from Eliot House who went on to Wadham, similar tales of a crucial kindness continued to be told : for example, of his making his way to dine in some simple flat with a Rhodes Scholar, married in his second Oxford year – he who might have dined anywhere. Accounts at the time of his death mentioned a political side of him that with another destiny might have carried him to the heights. In his enormous loyalty to Oxford and in what his sense of causes and persons led him to accomplish, such comments may have been natural, but to an outsider they were of the surface, not of the substance. It may seen paradoxical to say that he was a man of deeply inward commitments. His virtuosity – fascinating to others and (since everyone enjoys what he is good at) an art and amusement to himself – was essentially a shield. He would evade thanks or praise with some usually hilarious tale of how he had acted with cunning purpose. His was the opposite of Aristophanes' claim to have given up the old comic tricks in favour of useful ideas; he used his hilarity to protect his seriousness. And part of his seriousness was his feeling for people.

> κοιναὶ γὰρ ἔρχοντ' ἐλπίδες
> πολυπόνων ἀνδρῶν. ἐγὼ δ' Ἡρακλέος ἀντέχομαι
> προφρόνως
> ἐν κορυφαῖς ἀρετᾶν.

As the excellent obituary of him in *The Times* rightly concluded, sense of a political side of him was finally delusive because, interested though he was in the world, as in most things, it never occurred to him to be politic or, still less, to seek out other people than those who interested him or whom he liked. In essential modesty he doubtless never imagined that in his innumerable acts of benefaction he was doing anything of merit; he was simply standing with his friends.

He was at Harvard again in the college year 1948-9, as Charles Eliot Norton Professor, to deliver the later substance of his *The Romantic Imagination*, and this time lived in Eliot House where we by then were established, and we were in Oxford in 1954-5. He returned briefly for an honorary degree in 1963, and I stopped for a few days in Oxford in May 1969 to see him for what proved the final time; on a last Sunday morning we sat by the lawn of his Wadham garden watching a robin and discussing the *Odyssey*. We were both busier then, and there was less time for what in retrospect seemed those first Arcadian conversations, though there was still time; besides, many of his ideas were now written. This is not the place to try to describe his writing, but it was so integral a part of him as to prompt a few words if only for memory. Someone in Oxford singled out to me two flights of his, his memoir of Denniston to the British Academy and an address on Oxford to Rhodes Scholars, as most fully possessing the freedom and freshness of his conversation, and it was often said that his writing lacked the sparkle of his talk, as if to that extent it did not reflect him. But that is to assume that his marvellous gift for improvisation, humour, fancy, mimicry – that sudden mounting airiness that seemed as unforeseen to him as to his auditors – was his essential self. Doubtless it was a part of him, but underneath lay massive orderliness and rationality more suggestive of the age of Dr Johnson than of George VI. His *Heroic Poetry*, for example, is laid out in perspicuous areas of symmetrical mass. Details fit each division; he did not in a romantic spirit, not unakin to some impulses of scholarship, elaborate detail for itself but saw it as within a whole. His systematic working habits may have contributed, but steadiness and sanity of gaze were the decisive force; he felt the duty of clarity toward readers and still more toward the subject; for all his vitality, he did not wish to obtrude himself. His width of reading in many languages and literatures was a further force. Though Greek was his final love, he saw sentience and response to the world as very widespread, not the peculiar treasure of one age or culture, hence not to be unduly divided into academic subjects. In this sense too his mind showed a wide and essentially modest sanity, and its Palladian order, like its charity, was rather masked than revealed by the fountains of his conversation. It was a mark of his sanity that *Tradition and Design*, though from before the new understanding of oral composition, needed small adjustment to those ideas. Yet his gaze, though sane, was acute, and his wide and very persistent reading kept casting up flashes of implication; he read with intense awareness. As one among innumerable possible examples, his quotation in his late *Periclean Athens* (p. 160) may serve, of elegiac verses on the oracularly hinted but unforeseen and disastrous intervention of a demigod in the battle of Coronea in 447, which he used as commentary on the obscurely hinted outcome of the *Trachiniae* and *Oedipus Tyrannus*. His freshness and originality drew from the intensity of his reading. Yet the fact of his wide sanity remains; even at his most original he did not distort proportions; made his characteristic effects by fairness of estimate and purity of diction – or perhaps the effects just short of his finest, which the last chapter of his *Pindar*, called 'The Poetical Personality', may exemplify:

'Often enough gods and men are hopelessly severed, and, as the gods indulge in power and pleasure, men go their own faint and aimless way, but at times the whole situation is transfigured because the gods work in men to make them in some respects like themselves. In bringing them together song has much more to do than simply to announce a fact; it is itself an instrument by which men are made conscious of their closeness to the gods, and the gods are entreated to display their affection to men. With such duties to perform song must indeed have qualities of a very rare kind, and Pindar is confident that he possesses them through his intimate dependence on Apollo and the Muses. His innate, unquestioning pride in his poetical mission means that he gives to it all his gifts and all his efforts. The result is a poetry that by any standard deserves the name because it is based on a radiant vision of reality and fashioned with so subtle, so adventurous, and so dedicated an art that it is worthy to be an earthly counterpart of the songs which Apollo and the Muses sing on Olympus, and which Pindar regards as the archetype of music on those lofty occasions when all discords are resolved and all misgivings obliterated by the power of the life-giving word.'

The passage could not have been written by one who had not served like loyalties.

One more impression, as an outsider's, may seem eccentric to those who conceive him as long established in Oxford, an institution. As he says in *Memories*, his Shanghai childhood, trans-Siberian journeys between school and home, and abrupt shift to Flanders in the later stage of the First World War gave to his arrival at Oxford a tone almost of miracle. He never, I think, lost sense of that astonishing joy. Oxford remained to him a privilege that he expected to repay, the more because in childhood he had taken not even England for granted. Though he became a fine flower of the English education and admired its niceties, he was not in imagination essentially formed, much less confined, by these. His mighty virtuosity thus had a third source: it was not merely something that he did for fun and from extraordinary talent, not only a shield to protect deep inner feeling, it was what he owed Oxford and England. It was a personal counterpart to handsome towers and quadrangles and rooms, something that would not disgrace their beauty and style, a gesture of continuity and harmony, his due response. So conceived, his luminous flights were prompted by much the same impulse as inspired his services to the University as Warden, Vice-Chancellor, member of committees, and in countless unrecorded ways. He once said, perhaps not quite jokingly, that he wrote books because undergraduates liked having him do so. His

H

life was to an exceptional degree an act of loyalty – which is why other suggestions at the time of his death to the effect that he should have been a poet also seem mistaken. Not that he lacked the talent, but that he had in one sense a narrower commitment, to Oxford, in another sense a wider commitment, to all that the University implies: learning, writing, friends, the young, the flash and beauty of life, political freedom, intellectual standards, role in the nation. It was his acceptance of all these, to most minds mutually incompatible repayments that showed his great-heartedness. Many, perhaps most extraordinary men buy achievement at the price of drastic curtailment, but not he. He was a great man cast in the mould of the sustainers of the world, in the spirit of the Heracles of the metope at Olympia with Athena beside him.

11

Anthony Quinton

Maurice in America: II

Maurice did not altogether hold with America. He preferred things to be more manageable, more cut and dried. America was too amorphous and soggy for his taste, a vast, inadequately organised improvisation, in which the habitual reactions of intense cordiality make it all too clear that for most of the time nobody has the least idea of who anybody else is. His particular emblem for the defects was the performance of the public orator at, I think, Columbia University on the occasion when he was presenting Maurice for the award of an honoray degree. 'He brought off,' said Maurice, 'the unprecedented accomplishment of pronouncing all three of my names wrong.' 'I have the honour to present,' the orator had intoned, '*SEESUL MAWREECE BOE*RAH.'

All the same he spent two two-week periods with us in Long Island in the summers of 1969 and 1970, and on Sunday 4 July 1971 he was due to come to lunch with us to discuss the administrative details of a further visit that August (an extensive meal of Indian dishes was in preparation to promote the correct, far-flung frame of mind) when Stuart Hampshire, his successor at Wadham, rang up to tell us the sad news that Maurice had died early that day. I had been lucky enough to see a good deal of Maurice in Oxford in the preceding twenty years but there is no substitute, in the process of getting to know a person, for spending time with them continuously, in a domestic setting with all its small hazards and opportunities.

My wife has a number of general theories, of predominantly negative tendency, on the topic of Host and Guest. One, to which she would happily admit Maurice to be an exception, is that excellence in both capacities is almost impossible to obtain. In her view the difference is about as profound as that between the sexes. Hosts must be active, perceptive, striving creatures, constantly alert for the smallest indications of boredom or embarrassment, and, indeed, of hunger and thirst. Guests, however, are ideally contemplative, luxurious, even somewhat vegetable figures, happy to absorb whatever people, activities and nourishment may be set before them, capable of doing nothing at all contentedly for quite substantial periods and with no external ties whatever in the way of incoming telephone calls for which they have to be found, let alone untoward personal visitors. There is a corollary to her main thesis, however, which states that a small number of conspicuously good hosts are also good guests, and Maurice was highly placed in this group.

Another of her theories is that there is no correlation whatever between a person's general merits and likeableness and his qualifications as a guest. Some good people are bad guests; some bad people are good ones. How nice it is when, as with Maurice, both excellences coincide.

I had met Maurice quite soon after emerging from undergraduate life and going to reside in All Souls. Still single and with only rather generalised duties towards the advancement of learning, which could be discharged at times of my own choice, I was freely available to hang about for long periods after lunch or dinner revelling in, and making occasional suitably callow interruptions of, the conversational flow of the more entrancing guests. Thus I got to know Maurice, who made the quarter-mile trip from his lodgings in Wadham with agreeable frequency at the invitation of various colleagues. In due course I asked him to dinner myself.

Unfortunately the evening did not go quite as it should have. It was a week-day and only about ten people were dining, in the informal proximity of the common room. The party was of a size and nature Maurice would normally have more than held his own in, even brought under a genial form of centralised control. But one of the fellows had invited as his guest a slender, corvine Irish historian from T.C.D., whose combination of an unquenchable supply of anecdotes about Provost Mahaffy with a startlingly penetrating voice held Maurice impotently at bay. Once in a while, as the Irishman stopped to draw breath, Maurice would bark into action, but without effect. The star of the evening, perhaps deafened by the noise of his own contributions, would launch unheedingly into his next reminiscence. Maurice left early, soon after ten, with a somewhat congested look on his face. Our relationship was not soured by this mishap but it became, for a while, a little attenuated.

Around 1960, and now equipped with a family, I moved from a village some miles out of Oxford to a house belonging to my

college in Mansfield Road, just round the corner from the back
entrance to Wadham. Before long, fairly regular social relations
with Maurice were established. On our side these principally took
the form of Sunday lunch. These events had several properties that
Maurice appreciated, above all, perhaps, that of retaining their
essential features in an utterly regular way from one occasion to
the next. First, there would be large amounts of simple but un-
ashamedly calorie-bearing food, always enough for copious second
helpings. There would not be too many people, which had become
important for Maurice with increasing deafness. In the summer,
if the weather was good, we ate in the garden, well into the
afternoon.

Maurice would arrive at two minutes to one and down a plain
whisky. Essential items in our respective biographies since our last
meeting would be communicated. Then, with the announcement
of lunch, a more general spirit would prevail, scandalous truths
and falsehoods would fly about, and, as the beef or pork or lamb or
chicken went down, Maurice would say to my wife, 'Just what I
hoped for, dear girl.' The proceedings would close with the same
agreeable definiteness that they began with. We would escort Maurice round to the back door of Wadham. This being closed on
Sunday, he could let himself through a wicket gate with his key and,
once inside, would turn and briefly emerge with farewell and
thanks, looking, as a friend remarked, like the good-weather man in
an old-fashioned nursery barometer.

On his side he invited us to a series of dinners, usually in the
Lodgings. There would be from six to eight people. The first stage
was vodka, taken standing up in a small, dark room, filled with
books, just round to the left from the front door. At the meal itself
Maurice's attention would be at times slightly distracted by the
absolutely silent and, indeed, somewhat menacing-looking man
who passed the food. 'Bulgarian, of course,' Maurice would say if
he caught one's glance lighting on this taciturn man.

All tension was resolved when, with the business of eating completed, we moved up to the drawing-room and settled, or even
immersed, ourselves in its massively pneumatic armchairs and sofas.
There the conversation would broaden out to cover the great range
of Maurice's personal acquaintance over the years, the writers and
books that he knew about, which the rest of the company had at any
rate heard of. It has been said, in explanation of the comparative

flatness and impersonality of his written works, that he was unsure of himself. This unsureness did not extend to his capacities as a talker. He said a lot, very loudly, but he did not go in for monologues or hypnotic performances. Those with whom he talked were not Socratic feeds, confined to an intellectual analogue of 'Who was that lady you saw me with last night?' It was essential that those present should be egged on to saying things they did not know they had it in them to say. Maurice was a conductor as well as a soloist. When others piped up he showed the affectionate enthusiasm of a father watching his sons shine at a football match, not the impatience of an interrupted prima donna. Thus one tended to go home at the end of these evenings with a sense that this was really what it (the university, civilisation, even life) was all about.

In the early 1960s my wife's parents bought a house by the sea in East Hampton, Long Island for weekends and holidays. It became our custom to go there every year for the whole length of our children's summer holidays. The house was conceived on somewhat Edwardian and spacious lines, with a large number of small spare rooms in which we got friends from England to come and stay, usually, of course, people starting or finishing sabbatical years or summer schools in the United States. We were very gratified in 1969 when Maurice agreed to come over on a two-week excursion to stay with us.

On this first visit a policeman had been engaged to meet him at Kennedy airport and drive him out. In the late-August turmoil of that busy spot they failed to find each other and, as the telephoned communiqués of the policeman had reached a very doleful level, Maurice arrived on the doorstep, somewhat flushed, in his uncompromisingly English clothes. After what may be suspected to have been a short search for the driver who had been sent, he had, with Napoleonic resolution and despatch, hired a car for himself. The same readiness to make the best of things characterised his entire stay. He was soon attired in a white shirt and rather short khaki trousers and soon, too, he imparted a definite rhythm to the day.

Breakfast was taken early, downstairs, about five past eight. When my wife came down he liked to be given a clear account of the nature and timing of the day's social events. He then read until 11.30, abstaining from shopping forays into the village and declining offers to buy postcards for him on the ground that he did not know how to buy a stamp. At 11.30 he entered the swimming-pool,

getting out and diving in again a good deal. At 12.30 a brisk glass
of something was taken as an aspect of the drying process. He and
my father-in-law (his name too was Maurice) one day found a bottle
of kosher Czech slivovitz which was much to their taste. Each, to
excuse his further recourse to this attractive bottle, would use the
formula 'I'm just keeping Maurice company'. Lunch, of a picnic
style, would be eaten round the pool. Then Maurice would retire
to a comfortably-upholstered chair on the lawn in front of the
house, to 'read', an activity carried on with the eyes shut and the
book closed on the lap. At 4.30 another bout of swimming took
place, after which Maurice would go upstairs to bathe and array
himself for whatever the evening held in the way of a party or
going out to dinner.

As a swimmer Maurice was as brave as he was vigorous. The
swimming-pool has, near the shallow end, an orange plastic slide,
mounted by spindly metal steps, down which one could swoosh into
the water. It was most consistently used by the younger members
of the household. Maurice was determined to have a go. We felt
some concern as he quiveringly mounted to the top of the thing
and seated himself to survey the descent. 'I'm going over the top,'
he said. 'I'm trying to convince myself that the Hun can't stand
cold steel.' He propelled himself forward and disappeared in a
volcano of foam. Emerging from the water some distance away he
observed : 'It's just like being born.'

Maurice showed comparable enterprise in the matter of food.
The picnic-style lunch round the swimming-pool had as its central
element sandwiches with self-selected contents. Uncompromisingly
adult tastes were catered for with salami, cheese, liver sausage and
so forth. The children tended to stick to a particular very local
delicacy : sandwiches made with peanut butter, grape jelly and
marshmallow fluff, an extremely sweet, white, sticky substance. It
was not long before Maurice, asked to state his preference, would
say 'fluff for me, oh definitely fluff'. American butter is usually profoundly unsalted, but the refrigerator always contained some salted
butter, which was bought in two-pound plastic tubs. Seeing the
legend 'tub butter' on the side of this generous container Maurice
was at once reminded of the lines :

> Ladling butter from alternate tubs,
> Stubbs butters Freeman, Freeman butters Stubbs.

From then on 'Freeman and Stubbs, please' was his way of asking one to pass the butter.

In his later years Maurice was fairly deaf, and had acquired two neat but not all that effective hearing aids of the kind that clip on to the ear. At East Hampton these were put on, in a public and ceremonial way, when he came down in his evening wear after his bath. In the tuning process they ordinarily emitted high whistling noises. This rite, although agreeable in itself, did not seem to make any substantial contribution to Maurice's hearing, which appeared to vary in strength in accordance with inscrutable laws of its own. When it was not at its best he would fall back on creative improvisation. Sometimes this was simply a matter of answering 'Yerse, yerse'; sometimes, more committally, he would reply 'Wonderful, marvellous'; and occasionally splendidly inconsequential responses would emerge.

There is a good deal of social life at East Hampton in the summer, perhaps rather more than is strictly necessary for the mental health of all but the most doggedly gregarious. Maurice rose to these indiscriminate occasions magnificently. He was always very much himself, and yet quickly got on friendly communicative terms with the most varied and, as it were, unOxfordy kinds of person. In the United States an Oriental flamboyance of face, body and adornment is commonly the misleading cover for the simplest of hearts and the kindliest of natures. It was part of Maurice's humanity that he did not need to perceive this or work it out. For all his doubts about America he shared the American presumption that, in social life as much as in law, an individual is innocent until proved guilty.

Not that everyone he encountered on these occasions was wholly new to him. His immense range of friendships and acquaintanceships was revealed one evening at a large party in the neighbouring town of Southampton. Our host was a man distinctly sensitive to the fame or at least notoriety of the people he met, and he had assembled a very variegated and colourful collection of people on his lawn. Maurice, arriving in a sturdy Bulldog Drummond suit of hard-wearing material, introduced a negatively exotic note into the scene. Yet within a quarter of an hour he was the centre of a large and enthusiastic circle, containing indeed some unlikely Wadham men and the nieces or ex-daughters-in-law of learned or creative men known to him, but also a large infusion of enraptured new admirers, drawn by his unfailing power of making an event into an occasion. As we drove home my wife tentatively raised the question as to whether it might not be possible that our host dyed his hair. 'Dear girl,' said Maurice, 'it never crossed my mind that he didn't.'

There are various theories about the systematic principle underlying Maurice's jokes. If this variety in part reflects the selectiveness of memory, it must also reflect the marvellous variety of his performance. One friend chiefly recalls what may be called telegraphic antitheses: 'Queer as a coot; nobody minds' or 'Awful shit; never met him'. Most characteristic, however, are surely his reversed clichés. Of these a standard example is 'He's the sort of man who'd give you a stab in the front'. One I am particularly fond of refers to a distinguished person, noted for elaborate courtesy: 'I've just met So-and-so outside Blackwell's; he gave me the warm shoulder.'

The joke that to me incorporates in the neatest possible form the most of Maurice I heard at the end of a dinner given for him by the then Vice-Chancellor to mark, certainly not to celebrate, his retirement from the Wardenship of Wadham. It brings out his industriousness, his imaginative powers, his un-self-pitying sense of the passage of time. As they led the way out of the dining-room, passing my chair, I heard Allan Bullock say 'Maurice, would you like a pee?' 'No, no, dear boy,' said Maurice, 'given it up, waste of time.'

A personal reminiscence of Maurice, particularly one such as this, based on such a minute and fleeting foundation, must mention that the life-enriching splendour of his personality was associated, as such gifts seldom are, with extraordinary practical effectiveness. For a long period after the war he seemed to have become a kind of permanent Vice-Chancellor. The rule then prevailing for attainment of this office, that of seniority as head of a college, ensured that incumbents would usually come to it at a considerable age. Its immense burdens seemed equally calculated to ensure that these incumbents would soon collapse under them into ill-health. Maurice was always indestructibly ready to take up the load. How fortunate for Oxford that this was so, that someone so superbly humane, confident and imaginative was always at hand.

But more fundamental, I think, than either his enchantment of personality or his effectiveness in public action was his generosity. Maurice, to take this in the most concrete terms, was a great present-giver: imaginative, ample and frequent. When he moved out of the lodgings at Wadham his friends (and his friends' children) were showered with books and ornaments. As well as these testimonies of affection there was, too, a long history of large practical benefaction to people really in need of it. It is a great thing to have known him and for all those who did he is still very much alive when they find themselves saying, as we constantly do, 'How Maurice would have liked that.'

12

Kenneth Wheare

A Legendary Vice-Chancellor

My association with Maurice Bowra in university administration started in 1947 when I was elected to the Hebdomadal Council, of which Maurice had already been a member for some years, and lasted for twenty years until 1967 when we both decided not to stand for re-election on the ground, as Maurice said to me, that we and they had had enough. Maurice, having been elected Warden of Wadham in 1938, had by 1947 acquired considerable seniority as a head of a college, so that when at the beginning of the academic year in 1948 the sudden death of the then Vice-Chancellor occurred, and the head next in order of seniority, J. R. H. Weaver, President of Trinity, declined the office, Maurice would have succeeded in the normal course. But he was at Harvard and rightly preferred to fulfil his duties there and to postpone taking office as Vice-Chancellor, which he carried out in the years from 1951 to 1954.

Maurice's tenure of the office of Vice-Chancellor was legendary. Doing business with him was, of course, always a noisy experience. Enormous batches of business were dispatched at high speed and in a loud voice in the Hebdomadal Council and its committees. I think that the speed was, at times, too quick. Though people complain about the time taken up by committee work, they are not always grateful when it is reduced, particularly when it is reduced drastically. The normal duration of a meeting of the Hebdomadal Council in my time on it was a maximum of two hours; the standing orders assisted those who wished to bring business to a close at 4 p.m. and there was general agreement that stumps should be drawn in time for tea. Occasionally a meeting might go on till 4.30 p.m. and similarly a meeting might conclude at 3.30 p.m. These were the expectations. So when Maurice, in the early days of his Vice-Chancellorship, concluded the business at 2.10 p.m., or 2.30 p.m., or 2.45 p.m., some disgruntled men and women, with a sense of having been done out of something or other, were to be found descending the steps of the Clarendon Building, almost ashamed

to return to their colleges and face the colleagues who had felt
confident that they had said goodbye to them until tea time.

In fact Maurice, having demonstrated that he could wipe the
business out in a quarter of an hour, conformed to normal practice
quite soon, and there was little ground for complaint about business
being rushed. But in fact he liked to get it over. He did not really
enjoy the argument and in this respect was a complete contrast to
his successor as Vice-Chancellor, the Warden of New College,
A. H. Smith, his old tutor, who positively revelled in the discussion
of business. Where Maurice showed impatience with some member
of Council who was criticising or opposing some piece of business,
Warden Smith welcomed it, allowed the member to elaborate his
arguments in full, even assisted him in drawing out all their
implications, and then replied to them all point by point, so that,
at the end of perhaps half an hour, we were all back where we had
started; wiser, perhaps, but no further forward.

Maurice's view in general was that the business had already
been very fully discussed in a committee; it was set out in the
report; some exposition was needed; some questions might be asked
and answered; and then we should adopt it. On the issues which
came straight to Council and had not been considered by a committee, Maurice's practice as a rule was to say at the outset what
he thought should be done. Sometimes this worked well, but on
occasions he ran into trouble, and having nailed his colours to the
mast, he was in great difficulty in extricating himself. He was
cornered, fighting hard, lashing out in all directions, using a variety
of verbal weapons, including the bludgeon, as they happened to
come to hand. He did not like to be defeated in these encounters.
If one was occasionally and unfortunately on the wrong side when
the vote came, a charge of disloyalty might be preferred against
one. But it was an honour in a way, because it meant that you were
a friend and that he had thought highly of you and hoped that it
might be regarded as a temporary lapse.

It was said, as a criticism of Maurice as a chairman, that he was
more concerned with getting business decided than in getting it
decided rightly. Up to a point that was true; the exceptions were,
of course, those matters to which he was particularly committed.
Of Warden Smith, it was said, and correctly, that he was more
concerned to get the business decided his way than to get it decided.
For this reason I judged that Maurice was a much better Vice-

Chancellor than Smith. In general it seemed to me that, while a Vice-Chancellor, ideally, should be interested in the arguments that go on in the course of transacting university business, and capable of following them and of joining in from time to time, it is important that he should not be too interested, or too committed, and that he should remember that one of his tasks as a chairman is, if not to secure a decision, at any rate to secure a decision that there is to be no decision. He should be a moderator, not a partisan. Warden Smith was a partisan, quite apart from having a passion for argument and discussion. Maurice, in his impatience with discussion, got on with the business. If you wanted him to go slower, you could always stop him and ask for time, and it would be given, even if a little irritably. Generally speaking it is better to have a chairman who is going too fast, because you can usually slow him down, and you will get the support of your colleagues in doing so; if a chairman is going too slow and is enjoying every minute of it, it is practically impossible to hurry him up. This was the difference between sitting under the chairmanship of Maurice and that of Alick Smith. I used to think sometimes that it illustrated the difference between them in that Maurice was a scholar and Alick an intellectual. But that is perhaps too crude a distinction.

Though one is inclined to recall what Maurice did during his three-year term as Vice-Chancellor, it is worth remembering that he did an enormous amount of work as a member of committees of Council and of the General Board of the Faculties, the Curators of the University Chest, and as chairman of many committees of these bodies, as well as of faculty boards. The amount of detail involved in this work, little of it exciting, made it repugnant to many people, but Maurice tackled it as part of the job, devoting hours to preparing his agenda. You knew that, if such business could be transacted painlessly, Maurice could do it and hardly anybody else could. On the rare occasions when he was caught off guard by an unexpected point, or had failed to do his homework and found himself out on a limb, it was his custom, so the irreverent among us professed to believe, to declare rather gravely: 'I have given a great deal of thought to this. The point is by no means straightforward. There is a lot more involved here than meets the eye.' After one or two more sentences on these lines, Maurice would feel that he had got his bearings again and then announce his view.

In his last few years in University affairs, Maurice suffered from deafness and this made him less effective in the conduct of business and, of course, unpredictable in his interventions. On occasions he would speak when some other member was speaking, and of course, his stentorian voice tended to prevail; one sometimes doubted the veracity of his statement that he had not realised that someone else was speaking. Although he wore a deaf aid, he had a poor opinion of the achievements of medical science in the alleviation of deafness. On one occasion we were discussing a proposal in the Hebdomadal Council to establish a professorship of Otolaryngology. Maurice came to life suddenly. 'I advise caution in this field,' he said. 'In my experience I would say: Larynx – perhaps. Oto – Oh! No!' and he tapped his hearing aid as he said it. There was a bellow of laughter all round. Indeed nobody made Council bellow like Maurice, and it was usually beneficial.

To cope with his deafness he moved in the Hebdomadal Council to a seat opposite the Vice-Chancellor, which was advantageous to both parties. Maurice could follow better what was being said, sometimes with the aid of a little lip-reading, and he could also catch the Vice-Chancellor's eye if he wished to intervene. From the Vice-Chancellor's point of view it was an advantage to be able to keep your eye on Maurice and to speak direct to him. As a former holder of the office of Vice-Chancellor, Maurice was always careful to treat his successors with respect and consideration. He had a strong sense of the fitness of things. He could, of course, behave badly when he wanted to and occasionally when when he did not want to. But, in my experience, he never behaved badly towards his successors as Vice-Chancellor. In my own case this was a great relief and consolation, for I had a great affection for him and would not have liked to find myself in a position where I had to call him to order!

It was (and is, so far as I know) the custom to open the proceedings of the Hebdomadal Council each Monday with Prayers. The Collect: 'Prevent us, O Lord, in all our doings with thy most gracious favour . . .' was read by the Vice-Chancellor, to ensure (so progressives said) that no decisions were taken, and thereafter the Lord's Prayer, in which those members of Council who chose would join. When Maurice and I first joined Council it was the custom for almost all members to join in the Lord's Prayer, and some members indeed knelt down by their chairs for the whole of Prayers. But this last custom died out and at the same time the number of those joining, audibly at any rate, in the Lord's Prayer declined. Maurice was one of those who continued to join in, and of course was audible. When I was Vice-Chancellor I was always encouraged, at the beginning of a meeting, by his firm tones. I mentioned it to him one day, remarking how few still joined in. 'Not at all, old boy,' he said. 'Glad to give you a little ghostly comfort. Least I can do!'

Maurice was the last Vice-Chancellor to hold the office for three years until the Provost of Oriel (K. C. Turpin), 1966–9, after whom the present term of four years was established on the recommendation of the Franks Commission. Although Maurice's successors were certainly full-time holders of the office, in the sense that they devoted all their time to the job, none probably covered as wide a range of administrative affairs as he did, for he dealt with all the General Board business and seldom shed to pro-Vice-Chancellors any substantial block of important work. He served as acting-Vice-Chancellor for a period in 1959 during the illness of the President of Magdalen (T. S. R. Boase) and it fell to him to preside over the contested election for the office of Chancellor, when Mr Macmillan was chosen. Many enthusiastic alumni of the University who wished to qualify for the vote were required to take their M.A.s and Maurice greatly enjoyed the degree ceremonies at which this was done. His manner of tapping each candidate on the head with the New Testament while he recited the words '*In nomine Domini, Patris, Filii et Spiritus Sancti*' was thought by some to be too brisk and lighthearted and it was suggested by somebody that the whole ceremony should be 'de-Christianised' to accord with his lay approach. Maurice was indignant. 'I enjoy exercising my minor orders,' he said to me, 'and have no intention of giving them up for anybody.'

In the ceremonial and representational duties of Vice-Chancellor, which are still considerable at Oxford, Maurice was excellent. He took great trouble and he worked hard at it. If he turned up at a gathering he made his presence felt. I recall an address he gave in the Sheldonian to the assembled former Rhodes Scholars, celebrating in 1953 the Jubilee of the foundation of the Scholarships. It was eloquent, impressive, serious and inspiring, and it gave enormous pleasure to those who heard it. And this was done in the middle of an extremely busy period in his term as Vice-Chancellor.

To those who knew or know of Maurice as a witty speaker and a wildly entertaining talker, it might come as a surprise to know that he was, in University business and administration, a very serious man. He took himself seriously as an administrator and expected to be taken seriously. The business might be enlivened in the course of discussion, but it was not to be undertaken lightly or frivolously. In exposition he often sounded dull, adopting a monotonous emphatic tone. But, as I have said before, he got through it expeditiously. It was not always easy to predict what line he would take on any issue. The word 'monstrous' was a regular part of his vocabulary. In arguments with outside bodies, other universities, the University Grants Committee, he maintained always that Oxford was right, whatever he might say inside Oxford in criticism of what we were doing. This naturally did not make him popular in those circles. You had but to meet him on a deputation to the U.G.C. to realise what a uniquely Oxford man he was. The manner, the tone of voice, so familiar to us, was really an acquired taste. (Like certain wines, he did not export well.)

For my own part, I felt fortunate that he treated me as a friend. I felt also how fortunate we were in Oxford that a man of Maurice's academic distinction in literature and scholarship should be ready gladly to give so much of his time and energy to the business of university administration, with all its attendant boredom and frustration. But then university administration by university teachers is one of the guarantees of academic freedom, and Maurice had a passionate belief in academic freedom.

13

Mortimer Wheeler

Maurice Afloat, and as P.B.A.

There was one subsidiary aspect of Bowra's interests and activities of which something must be said if our picture of him is to approach completeness. I have in mind his devotion to Mediterranean cruising. It was indeed a fortuitous encounter on a Hellenic cruise-ship that, many years ago, brought us together in what was to become an enduring friendship. Previously, fortified no doubt by the latent snobberies of a conventional classic education, I had very rarely ventured upon those somewhat miscellaneous and parcelled exploits; but now on the instant all petty inhibitions were swept to the sea-winds. I still recall the first day on which, as I approached the main deck, a deep voice – the voice of conviction and of laughter – was wafted towards me above the normal tumult of the ship's bar. And there was Maurice, in the midst of a small, attentive coterie of the sort of intelligentsia that these rather well-conditioned cruises were liable to attract, exuding contentment of a highly articulate and widely various kind. For the moment, I admit, the situation gave me a little to wonder. But I soon learned to value Maurice's exuberance as that of an overflowing mind fed torrentially from sources as diverse as Pindar and Pushkin and in its course shaping channels no less diverse through a multitude of lesser intelligences sufficiently united by quick comprehension and ready argument. In a way, I occasionally found myself with a secret smile regarding him, in this guise, as a peculiarly lovable sophist, stimulated by a genuine joy alike in learning and in the easy communication of the market-place.

In more formal moments on shipboard or ashore he gave to what may be called tour-lecturing a new status, which in turn attracted to these cruises other scholars of not incomparable professional attainment, men and women of learning and curiosity sometimes capable also of adapting their wares to the taste of the lay consumer – a duality not always easy to discover; surprisingly few specialists, it seems, can transmit imaginatively. But in both fields Bowra was

I

both master-mind and mobile model; with the compensating faculty
of losing himself from time to time with a Greek dramatist in
some obscure shade, or of plunging vaguely clad and porpoise-like
into the summer sea. Or again in those sunlit mornings when he
and I might evade the crowd and spend a peaceful hour or two
of miscellaneous talk in some remote taberna where we knew the
local wines and interlaced them with the fruits of the sea as the
homeward boats arrived intermittently at the quay.

As President of the British Academy

In 1958 Bowra became President of the British Academy, of which
I was at the time Honorary Secretary, and our association assumed
official facets which I have described elsewhere.[1] Whether as
President or as recurrent Vice-Chancellor of his University, Bowra
fulfilled his offices with undisguised gusto and devotion. Early in
our official association I found myself transferring to him Pope's
apostrophe to Swift:

> Whether thou choose Cervantes' serious air,
> Or laugh and shake in Rab'lais' easy chair,
> Or in the graver gown instruct mankind,
> Or, silent, let thy morals tell thy mind

– words from which I would not perhaps press a pedantic appli-
cation of the last line. But of Rabelais there was with no doubt at
all more than a casual trait.

Two episodes added lustre to his four-year Presidency. When he
entered upon his term, he took over from his predecessor, Sir
George Clark of Oriel, the Chairmanship of an Academy committee
recently established in consultation with and at the charge of the
Rockefeller Foundation for the purpose of preparing a survey of
the existing organisation in the United Kingdom of research in the
studies represented by the Academy, with special reference to
the public and private sources of financial support. In other words
it would cover the humanities and the social sciences as subjects
of higher study much as the natural sciences were covered by the

---

[1] *The British Academy 1949–1968*, particularly pp. 47, 78, 84, 151–2.

Royal Society. Incidentally attention would be paid to parallel problems and provision in countries overseas.

Details of this considerable enterprise are available elsewhere; for example, in *The British Academy 1949–1968* already cited. Here it will suffice to remark that Bowra steered the enquiry with wisdom and ardour, and after eighteen meetings the resulting *Report on Research in the Humanities and the Social Sciences* was published in February 1961. Its main contentions were at once accepted by H.M. Treasury, and in his final Presidential Address to the Academy on 11 July 1962 Bowra was able to announce a substantial Government grant on an annual basis for the maintenance and development of research in the Humanities – the first definitive grant of the kind in the history of Treasury benefaction.

The work begun with so much acumen by Sir George Clark in the last days of his Presidency was thus brought to a triumphant conclusion almost on the last day of Sir Maurice Bowra's vigorous tenure of that office. It had been a happy episode with a happy and fructuous ending.

The second outstanding episode of Bowra's Presidency was the establishment of a flourishing British Institute of Persian Studies at Teheran. For the general context in which this major operation took shape it will suffice to recall briefly the gradual pervasion and development of organised British scholarship overseas before 1960.

As far back as 1885, in what may be dubbed the Schliemann-Gladstone era, a British School of Archaeology had been founded at Athens and had gradually attracted a modest income from private and public sources. In other words it had acquired a recognised place in the academic and indeed the social Establishment of the later Victorian epoch, and was a proper precedent for the addition of a British School in Rome at the turn of the century. The new Roman School was able, with the help of the 1851 Exhibition Commissioners, to extend its scope in 1911 to include students of Architecture and the Fine Arts, and to the present day, amidst intermittent disputation, uniquely retains these wider functions. In 1919 a British School of Archaeology, at first more in name than in fact, was founded in Jerusalem; and this new eastward trend was carried further in 1932 when, as a memorial to the life and work of Gertrude Bell, a British School of Archaeology in Iraq arose at Baghdad. Sixteen years later, at the end of the Second World War, this Asian salient was broadened by the inauguration of a British

Institute of Archaeology at Ankara, and a dozen years later still the British Academy successfully opened new regions to research in what were then the British Colonial Territories of East Africa.

Meanwhile an organised effort was made by the dying Raj to bring the Archaeological Survey of India into line with European standards, and this process may be said to have reached an appreciable stage of advancement when India achieved independence in 1947. The Indian Survey had of course no organic connexion with the British Schools which I have catalogued, but its aims and standards were of a comparable kind, and it may be claimed that there was now a significant unison of approach to archaeological studies under Western encouragement from the Mediterranean to the Bay of Bengal. Only in one part of that huge area was there still a gap of any momentous extent – momentous both geographically and historically. I refer to the interval represented by Iran and Afghanistan. In both of these kingdoms important work had been done for several decades under French leadership, but the developing technologies which were peculiarly characteristic of the parallel British institutions had not yet taken firm root there.

Accordingly when in 1959 a tentative impulse became evident in Iran itself for the promotion of some sort of British Institute as a counterpart of the Institut Français at Teheran, the opportunity (if such it was) was difficult to ignore. On the other hand from the Academy's point of view the moment was peculiarly inopportune. The new British Institute in East Africa was just struggling to its feet and required careful nursing by its academic parent. And Bowra was up to the eyes on the preparation of the vitally important Rockefeller Report on Research. For a time the Secretary, in consultation with the British Council, carried on behind the scenes such negotiation with Iran as was feasible at long range.

By the middle of 1960, however, our Iranian negotiators were putting forward proposals which clearly called for consultation at closer quarters. Moreover the Rockefeller operation was by now drawing towards its end, and the Academy had more time for other business. Further, if anything was to be done it was evident that the British State Visit to Teheran, announced for March 1961, would necessarily enter into the picture. Bowra, now fully apprised of the whole situation, threw himself into the fray. He and I had both been gunners; backed by the Foreign Office, we would descend upon Teheran and open fire together.

Again details are recorded elsewhere. Our Teheran episode was a lively one, culminating in attendance upon the Shahanshar, both Bowra and I encased breathlessly in resistant morning-dress as in ancient suits of armour. The Imperial blessing was readily given to our proposed British Institute, and was followed by an entertaining Imperial monologue on the unhappy state of the non-Iranian world at large. We withdrew, murmuring appropriate platitudes on the virtues of cultural interchange, and were welcomed with open arms to the academic and diplomatic hospitality of the Capital.

At home our reception was no less gratifying. The Financial Secretary of the Treasury, again backed by the Foreign Office, supplied the necessary funds; and the new British Institute of Persian Studies was duly acknowledged in March at Teheran by the Queen and Prince Philip. In December of that year the ceremonial inauguration took place in the presence of Maurice Bowra, the Rector of Teheran University, and the Iranian Minister of Court. The Institute was in fact already hard at work.

One further point of developing interest may be observed in the present context. The earlier British Schools and Institutes, for which the British Academy now sustained a general responsibility to Government, had, with the partial exception of the School at Rome, been specifically and almost exclusively concerned with Archaeology. The new Institute of Persian Studies claimed a far more comprehensive field. From the outset Bowra rightly emphasised that it was no less interested in Persian art and literature – in Persian humanism as a whole – than in the architecture and buried vestiges of the more conventional and limited scholastic tradition. This widening concept of the function of British Schools and Institutes overseas, if not wholly due to Bowra, certainly owed much to his active participation in the broad Persian project during its formative period and is beginning, retrospectively, to lend a liberal re-thinking to the functions of some of the older foundations. The attribute 'liberal' is not the least of those which I should like in this brief memorial note to attach to Maurice Bowra's memory.

14

Leslie Mitchell

An Undergraduate's View of the Warden

In some ways, I suppose, I was one of the most practised under-graduates ever to come up to Oxford. Indeed, the whole process of 'coming up' simply involved five minutes by car to Wadham. I had been born in the city. I had been educated there. At the time of my arrival at Wadham in 1962, I had never been outside Oxford for more than two weeks, and then only to make short excursions for family holidays on the south coast. Before starting on a formal undergraduate career, I had made a ten-day visit to Paris, and had, in truth, found that tolerably exciting, but to claim that my intel-lectual and geographical horizons were anything but narrow would be going too far. Somehow, if reading was to be enjoyed anywhere, it was to be enjoyed *here*. At all times, it was to be preferred to other kinds of experience.

My expectations of the University were therefore enormous. If Oxford schoolmasters were by definition clever, the Oxford don must be a truly wonderful creature, and the Head of an Oxford college semi-divine. Certainly the University's public face was breathtakingly impressive. Long before coming up, I knew about sub-fusc, May morning and the Schools. During Eights Week, I knew which barge belonged to which college, and very quickly began to develop preferences. Like any conscientious tourist, I visited each of the colleges in turn during the school holidays. Chapels, halls and gardens fell into place as I read up the history of the society concerned. If undergraduates were encountered in Grimbly Hughes or the Cadena, they all seemed uniformly bril-liant and occasionally irritating. They were clearly the predestined inhabitants of some better and brighter world.

Evidence of a rather more concrete kind was provided at a school prize-giving in the mid-fifties, when it was announced that that year's speaker was to be the Warden of Wadham. The negotiating of the High Street was always considered to be something of an adventure by Maurice, and we were conscious of the fact that some kind of special honour was being accorded to the school. I remember being struck by a sense of disappointment that such an obviously great man should, at first sight, appear so small, and, from a schoolboy's point of view, be so amazingly round. The sheer energy in the figure as it strode towards the platform, however, smothered any temptation on the part of an irreverent body of schoolboys to laugh. When that bittern-booming voice, amplified by microphones, began to fill the Town Hall, we knew that it would have been very unwise to have done anything of the sort.

The details of the speech he made on that occasion have long since been forgotten, but one point does stand out in my memory. When he made all the conventional remarks about the value of games and the worthiness of those who had *not* won prizes, I had the distinct impression that he did not mean it. Just as obviously, the handing over of books to those who had been lucky enough to win them gave him enormous pleasure. He shook hands and said 'splendid' as only he could, plunging into what seemed like five minutes of inward reflexion on the first syllable, and then pulling out of it with a snap on the second. He studied the titles of the books we had chosen with care, and, when he saw that I had opted for *A Tale of Two Cities*, he winced. My image of a Head of House was confirmed. This was something strange and Olympian.

All the above needs to be mentioned by way of preface to explain the context in which the breaking down of the Oxford myth occurred for me on taking up residence. I discovered that not all my contemporaries were by definition cleverer than me. In fact, it has to be said that some of them were quite definitely less so. Dons turned out to be people who talked about quite ordinary things quite often. They did not appear to be obsessed by the vintage of clarets, and such eccentricity as there was could not cause any kind of disquiet. None of them had beards. Like every undergraduate who has ever entered the University, I underwent, in my first two terms, that process of rediscovering Oxford in its own terms which is an essential precondition of enjoying it to the full. Only one element in the situation measured up to the schoolboy image of the place, and that was Maurice Bowra. He did seem impossibly clever, and never talked of ordinary things.

In the first two terms of each new academic year, the Warden invited all the Freshmen to dinner in relays on Sunday nights. He regarded this as the duty of a Head of House, and had nothing but contempt for his colleagues in the University who contented themselves with mass sherry parties. He worked through the college quite methodically. It became reasonably easy to predict when one's turn would come, and, by outlining this sequence, it was simple to impress junior members of the college with one's knowledge of the workings of the Senior Common Room. Week by week, the Wadham Freshmen reported to the Lodgings in the following order: major Scholars in the arts subjects; minor Scholars in the arts subjects; major science Scholars; minor science Scholars; the arts Commoners; and finally the science Commoners.

Such an ordering inevitably laid the Warden open to the charges of being an intellectual snob and a contemner of science. I am sure that he would have readily pleaded guilty to the first. He faithfully attended the last day of both the Torpid and Eights race weeks, although he freely admitted that he had never mastered the rules of these events, and was quite often to be seen bellowing encouragement to the wrong crew. He also once observed that, having fought in one World War and having done his best to avoid another, it was hard to understand what the purpose of it all was if it could not even result in the abolition of rowing. All exercise should be entirely cerebral. Even though the end result might be character destruction rather than character formation, the Warden would probably have claimed that certain types of character should never be built anyway. He would have found incomprehensible the argument that a mountain should be climbed because it was there, but would have argued the same point vigorously with regard to the novels of Jane Austen or George Eliot.

As for the problem of the sciences, which really only came to maturity as firm disciplines in the Warden's Oxford lifetime, I think he felt some embarrassment. Here were highly important areas of knowledge about which he knew little. The language of the scientist was one of the few he could not understand. His caustic, and not unalloyed, respect for Cyril Hinshelwood stemmed from a formal, academic appreciation of a mind that could successfully straddle the arts/science divide. For someone like the Warden who lived to talk, a problem of language or a hitch in communication could be excruciating. Literary and historical anecdotes, or the kind of dinner party game that involves finding all the nice people in Proust, could clearly not carry impact for people involved in very different disciplines. There is no point in trying to apportion responsibility for this kind of estrangement. Quite simply, in the twenties, the best minds were automatically drawn to Greats, and, occasionally, to History or P.P.E. Now some of them preferred to tackle Physics or Physiology. The adjustment was rather hard to make.

Accordingly, on the first Sunday of my academic career, I, together with five other arts men, presented myself at the door of the Lodgings and rang the bell. As may be easily imagined, the sense of expectation on that occasion was enormous. Strangely though, that same sense of expectation recurred whenever that door opened for dinner over the next ten years. The nearest analogy would be that of entering a theatre. There was to be a performance. There was quite clearly a leading actor. But, if the evening was to be a success, the audience also had to be in good form. References had to be taken, and the subtlest of innuendoes acknowledged. If the flow of wit showed the slightest sign of drying up, in itself a most unusual occurrence, it was easily regenerated by one of the audience making a comment or inquiry about any of the leading political or literary figures of this century. It was rather like serving tennis-balls to a professional, who then proceeded to smash and lob characters all over the court, or send them lovingly and gently down the line.

Others can speak with more authority about the development and intricacy of the Warden's conversation. From the undergraduate's point of view, its range and sheer cleverness was stunning. I do not think some of us ever quite recovered from a first exposure to its impact. Quite simply, the Warden seemed to know every language in the world, and therefore, when making some general point about poetry or literature, he could draw on his familiarity with Chinese, Portuguese, Russian, Italian and Greek, both ancient and modern. It would be assumed that the more familiar languages would be known as a matter of course. There was no book that we knew of on which the Warden could not offer some comment or anecdote. What was more important, he always assumed that, if someone admitted that they had never read any Schiller or Balzac, this was solely the result of a lack of time and never of any want of inclination. There was never any condescension therefore. Rather he talked to undergraduates as fellow members of a club, whose common preoccupation was a devotion to books and to all kinds of literature in particular. Some of the club's members were older and more experienced, but that alone distinguished them. Therefore, although the Warden's conversational style towards undergraduates was of necessity in the form of a monologue, it contained the intimation of an appeal to some kind of equality, and was in some sense flattering.

Just as surprising for the newly-arrived undergraduate was to hear someone speaking familiarly about people who for us were already historical characters. The Warden seemed to have met, conversed with or known rather well everyone of note this century. The Oxford of the inter-war years was obviously something of a special subject for him, and Evelyn Waugh and his contemporaries emerged at first hand. More surprisingly, Henry James had asked him how he liked Cheltenham. He had disliked the spartan living of Bloomsbury, but had revelled in the more high-spirited and wordly weekends at Ottoline Morrell's Garsington. Predictably, he had disliked Goebbels. Equally predictably, he had sympathised with Valéry when he was asked to play bowls after dinner at All Souls. His description of Cocteau's real or pretended claustrophobia playing havoc with the domestic arrangements of the Randolph Hotel was a tour de force. He had heard Chaliapin sing Boris Godunov, and he had seen Karsavina dance The Firebird. He had known Petrograd between the February and October Revolutions, and he had visited Berlin in the thirties. Story after story tumbled out, spiced, pointed and, it must be said, occasionally elaborated. No dinner-table of undergraduates could fail to be captivated.

On this first encounter, those of us who were seated across the table from the Warden had most opportunity to become acquainted with his extraordinary manner of speech. A large bowl of flowers almost entirely obscured our view of the Warden, and we could only catch glimpses of him through leaves and petals. The impact of the voice was therefore all the more compelling. Its cadences were extraordinary and wholly original. It rose and fell in the most surprising way, and, once the Warden had told a story, it would be unthinkable, and probably impossible, to repeat without doing so with his rhythm and emphasis. What humour there was in the remark that Neville Chamberlain 'looked less like a banana than an umbrella' lay in the fact that the first two syllables were enunciated with the speed of a rifle shot while the last stretched away to infinity. This unique style was an integral part of his conversation and wit, which quite often cannot be understood unless spoken in the same voice. Its effect on his rendering of the first fourteen verses of the first chapter of St John's Gospel, which he read at the end of every carol service, was quite extraordinary. On only one occasion was this personal style modified. He decided to read Yeats aloud at the end of a dinner party, and the poet himself, who had known Wadham well, had instructed him in the appropriate rhythms.

Such dinner parties always ended promptly at ten thirty. As soon as the Wadham Tompion had struck that hour, guests were politely, but firmly, ushered towards the door. The Warden's assumption was that he had an overwhelmingly busy day in the offing, and that we were in the same position. In truth, it has to be said that this was always true for him and less so for us. It helped to make the point, however, that such evenings should be the necessary relaxation at the end of a fully productive day, and not simply the stylish culmination of idleness. He worked ferociously hard himself, and expected his colleagues and undergraduates to do the same. Not to do so was somehow to demonstrate a gross ingratitude for whatever intellectual abilities one had been given. He genuinely liked people to win Firsts. He really disliked the squandering of talent for any reason other than that of personal misfortune, with which he would always sympathise. He deplored what he took to be the English schools' habit of discouraging the overt, and perhaps tiresome, expression of 'cleverness'. He believed very firmly in the supremacy of intellectual values above all others, based on hard work and a careful reading of the texts.

In the course of the next ten years, this image of the Warden necessarily underwent certain modifications, but its fundamental constituents never varied. The same preoccupation with intellectual values predominated. If he lent a book, this would involve the recipient in the preparation of a formal opinion that would be listened to with care and interest. He would be genuinely shocked by someone preferring *Le Rouge et le Noir* to *La Chartreuse de Parme*. At no time, however, would he allow his basic kindness to be overborne. His representation of academic values was the more magnetic because it was accompanied by personal acts of generosity and civilised behaviour. A very large number of Wadham men would be able individually to bear witness to this fact. It was clear

that he took a personal pleasure in seeing his friends prosper and
in a position to be happy. Towards the end of his life, the dependence on this circle of friends grew greater. The younger members
of that circle were almost his intellectual creations, and he was
obviously very pleased that they should continue to look to him
for support and encouragement.

This outpouring of generosity and kindness demanded in return
a certain measure of personal loyalty. There was no more terrible
adjective in the Warden's vocabulary than 'disloyal'. To be accused
of such a thing was to fall under the most terrible of anathemas.
It would, however, be hard to detail the exact constituents of the
canon which could not be transgressed. Inevitably, there were
certain figures about the University whom no right-thinking man
could, according to the Warden, possibly admire or respect. To be
impressed by them might suggest a lack of sensitivity therefore.
Equally, I think the Warden would have been much surprised if
one of his friends had decided to take up weight-lifting before
breakfast. Disloyalty on points of academic detail was a less serious
offence, although, on one occasion, a rather over-fussy and humour-
less defence of Zola was cut short by the invocation of this word.

Somewhere too, a loyalty to Oxford and its idea of a university
was involved. He believed that colleges were for undergraduates
and that it was impossible to take too much trouble over them. He
accepted the growth in graduate studies with pleasure, but once
characterised the graduate as a kind of dinosaur sinking under the
weight of his narrow learning into some primaeval bog. Scientists
were a little suspect, because of necessity their work involved them
being out of college for long periods. On being offered a Fellowship at another college, I was treated to a formal lecture on what
the responsibilities of a don actually were. He conceived of them
almost in terms of a mission, and talked of 'saving' people from
what he regarded as the deplorable narrowness and philistinism of
the English social system. Loyalty and disloyalty, therefore, had
nothing whatever to do with social class. Rather, they were ideas involved with subscription by individuals to articles of faith concerning the University and its purpose.

Inevitably, as he grew older, loyalty came to be described in
more closely personal terms. The last dinner party he gave in the
Warden's Lodgings before giving up that office was a very difficult evening for him. The Warden was simply not the sort of

person to surrender a position or give up any kind of battle easily. Indeed, the whole idea of retirement at a given age was to be regarded as a weakness of mind. He had directed the affairs of Wadham for over thirty years, and he looked upon it with absolute justice as his own creation. On this particular evening, he was unusually funny about the subject of retirement. One remembered how delighted he was to quote Henry James's remark on death: 'So here it is at last, the distinguished thing!' Basically, however, leaving the Lodgings was a major – perhaps the major – upheaval in his life, and I sometimes think he never quite adjusted to it.

On this evening too, there was a great deal of talk about the physical problems involved in removing from one part of the college to another. The promise that a squad of volunteers would be formed to deal with the books settled one problem, and this was duly done. There were other problems that were more intractable, however. The works department had expressed doubts on the question of whether the ceiling of the rooms into which the Warden was moving could bear the weight of a large chandelier. Equally galling was a suggestion that the Warden's desk could in no way be manoeuvred through the narrow doors of the new building. All these questions were resolved satisfactorily in the end, but at the time they obviously caused real and deeply felt distress. For the first time in many years, the Warden was brought up against problems of a purely practical nature outside the cushioning effect of the college system.

This rather trivial incident served to emphasise the extent to which the Warden was the product of pre-First World War society and of the Oxford-between-the-Wars. Financially and professionally secure, it allowed the cultivation of a spirited intellectual and personal independence, which sometimes drifted towards eccentricity. It was a world of servants, and college life was comfortable and well-regulated. When the Head Scout in Wadham reported the death of a Fellow to the presiding Fellow at dinner, he was told, in a matter-of-fact voice, to inform the Domestic Bursar. Equally, it was a system which had no need of the constricting restraints of the thesis and the doctorate, and the committee was kept within proper limits. Fellows of colleges read widely, and could develop academically in many directions. There seemed to be a kind of intellectual *douceur de vivre*, which has drained steadily away ever since. Maurice Bowra was very much a product of this system. His breadth of learning, style of wit and magnificent erudition developed in these very special conditions. As a result, it is possible to say, with the deepest sense of loss, that there will never again be anyone quite like him.

In essays of this kind, there is almost a convention that somewhere mention should be made of someone influencing someone else. The precise, personal chemistry of this process is always hard to pin down, and it is perhaps wise to be cautious about the whole concept. In the case of Maurice Bowra, however, the effort has to be made if justice is to be done to his character. His influence simply stemmed from his being the cleverest and funniest man one had ever met. In a strange way too, although he had spent most of life behind college walls, he was also one of the most widely-lived. His influence was couched in benign and generous terms. For many of us, it was a decisive factor in our lives.

Susan Gardiner

Maurice at Dinner

On a table lay the note: an invitation to dinner, 7.30, 8 July, day clothes. Moments of pleasurable anticipation would have enlivened those preceding hours: the certainty of the courteous welcome, the sudden affectionate hug, the powerful grip on the arm as one was led to the vodka. And then, around the table, the gradual relaxation as the reverberating voice took command, tossing stories like cards, revealing the rise and fall of kings and their courts, displaying triumphantly the concealed joker . . . Instead, on that July afternoon, the funeral service over, a dazed and straggling line of mourners halted in the college quadrangle. The familiar buildings, serene in the hot sun, watched as the coffin was carried through the entrance. Opposite and apart, framed by an archway, the solitary figure of a poet leant wearily upon a stick, he also soon to die. Only then did the realisation of this death overwhelm. There had been no Boswell to record and evoke the famous conversation and now – besides the sorrow, almost an anger, at the personal loss – there came the wider regret that new generations, of which one is so peculiarly aware in Oxford, could never be touched by so liberating a spirit.

I remembered when I first met him. To me, twenty years old, and coming to Oxford from outside, the University appeared at first a bewildering society, criss-crossed with divisions like an ancient face. There was the initial separation of persons into their colleges, and then into rank, subject and degree: friendships obviously overruled the lines but, even so, the questions seemed inevitably to be asked – where is he from, what does he do, by whom was he taught? And then, compounding all, what age, what year? – an alarming docketing, as if these facts must be elicited before the foundations of knowing could be considered secure, an opinion divulged. To come thus – ignorant of the customs, fearful of the questions or (worse) the lack of them, mistaking kind interest for criticism and never quite sure where fiction ended

and reality began – was to find even an everyday dinner party a
dreaded ordeal where one might nervously bare one's soul or else
remain defiantly, childishly, silent. I had, of course, been told about
Maurice beforehand – photographs had been shown, his voice
mimicked, his achievements noted, and there were the shelves of
his writings. But how could one really have known what to expect?
Entering a North Oxford drawing room, there above all was the
sound of the voice, more resonant, more pervasive, than imaginable;
but there, too, was a formidable group of people locked in those
almost painful silent contortions of laughter usually only witnessed
– if the seconds can be spared to look round – at a Marx Brothers
film. The cause of this scene rose, quickly but jerkily, from an
armchair, hand outstretched to welcome; a short, top-heavy figure.
Portraits had concentrated, and with justice, on the strength of
the weighty sculpted head; but why had they so astonishingly
neglected the passion and piercing intensity of the eyes?

As the evening went on and I learnt to distinguish the words
behind the voice – it was as if English played normally by the
piccolos were suddenly taken over by the bassoon – I began to
realise, not only that I had forgotten my apprehensions, but that
here was a person in whose presence those around him lost artifice
or pomposity and that the complexities of this strange society were
no end in themselves but only a necessary, sometimes surprisingly
amusing, means to an end. It was then that I first heard Maurice's
often quoted remark, on being asked the age of a person under
discussion – 'Oh, *our* age, *our* age . . .', accompanied by a wide
sweep of the arm to make clear to everyone present that it included
them, whether eighteen years old or eighty. This remark, at first
comic with all its implications, could also be oddly comforting,
underlining as it did that the barriers of age need not be such
obstacles after all. For Maurice did not look upon the condition
of youth as if it were some type of disease to be treated as quickly,
as effectively, as possible. With him there seemed to be no need for
a constant appeal to memory to revive sympathy for the young; he
had a natural spontaneous understanding which was never patron-
ising, encouraging rather than stifling the tenderest aspirations.
Under his influence – notwithstanding the satirical remarks, the
occasional malice, the delight in drama – one invariably felt a
greater warmth towards one's fellow humans, a recognition of the
pettiness of so many of one's personal concerns. And this remains.

At his best he could stir and awaken the faintest hidden spark of talent: his own innate love of language and the particular word marked the hidden poet. Though quick to dismiss the charlatan, the sycophant, his loyalty to his friends seemed unshakable. When on one occasion guests, gossiping about some colleague, had descended from the amusing to the vicious, Maurice – roused – cut through with a brisk 'Yes, yes, he is a monster, but we all love him, don't we?' We didn't, but we were chastened, perhaps even persuaded to feel grateful that monsters were not extinct.

One evening in Wadham I was taken by Maurice into dinner. There – possibly over-stimulated by the introductory vodkas and the ambience of the hall – I confidently embarked on a complicated defence of some of the works of Katherine Mansfield with two people who, I decided, were unappreciative of their excellence. By forgotten ways one of Hardy's novels came to be similarly involved. Maurice, meanwhile, was watchful and unusually silent – so much so that I feared he was displeased. After the coffee and the ensuing formalities were over, my arm was taken in the familiar firm grasp and I was led away. The evening should not have ended so soon: Maurice must, I thought sadly, be bored and tired. Into the Lodgings – but no, not for the coat and wrap. I was quietly taken upstairs and, bemused, invited to sit down while he, two books in his hands, began reading: first a poem of Yeats, then several by Thomas Hardy – for which the book was unnecessary, his eyes rarely needing the reminding words. No comment was made and none was expected. I was taken down to the door with characteristic courtesy and, in spite of the icy rain of a winter's night, led through the quadrangle and the gate to the road and my car.

Two mornings later the long gaunt village postman, his uniform glinting with melting snowflakes, knocked at the window. In his hands was a ruffled parcel, the string awry, the paper loosened. As the frayed wrappings were removed, a note fluttered down from the enclosed book.

'. . . Here is poor Jude,' it said, 'a bit shaky but in his first form.'

K

16

Francis King

'Pray You, Undo this Button'

'Did you know Maurice Bowra well?'
'Well, I did once take down his trousers.'

The time was the early fifties; the place, Mandra – one of those
dusty Greek villages that have the appearance of having been
nibbled at by generation after generation of goats and scratched
over by generation after generation of chickens. We were on our
way back from a weekend visit to Delphi. It had been decided by
the British Embassy and the British Council that, after a week of
giving lectures and attending parties, Maurice 'could do with a
rest'; but I suspect that it was not he but his hosts for whom the
rest was needed. People who are themselves indefatigable at first
stimulate but then fatigue others.

In the car on our return journey – the other passengers were
Alethea Hayter, then a member of the British Council like myself,
Brian de Jongh and a British chauffeur – Maurice had for some
reason been holding forth on the subject of ages at which it was
fashionable to die. 'No, you're at quite the wrong age, Alethea.
You've left it too late and now you'll have to hang on for several
years more. But Francis is at exactly the right age. He couldn't
choose a better one.' He began to enumerate all the famous writers,
composers and painters who had died at the same age as I then
was – Shelley, I remember, was one of them.

We had had a heavy and indigestible luncheon, preceded by
quantities of *ouzo* and accompanied by several carafes of *retsina*
('exactly like hospital bottles' Maurice had said of these carafes
and had then made a clinical comparison between what we were
drinking and what hospital bottles might contain), so that in the
middle of his list of names I dropped off to sleep. I was woken by
what I at first took to be a violent punch on the nose, as a lorry,
hurtling round a hairpin bend on the wrong side of the road,
ploughed into our car. I had been flung forward at the impact and
what had, in fact, struck me was not Maurice's fist but the back

of his seat. The driver appeared to be unconscious. Maurice emitted a series of hollow, horrifying groans, like an elephant in rut or labour, and then also passed out. I staggered out of the car, looked down at my shirt and, seeing that it was saturated with blood, assumed that I had been seriously injured. Overcome by faintness, I lay down in a ditch. Within seconds an elderly woman, swathed from top to toe in black – the mother, it later transpired, of the lorry-driver – was screeching abuse at me in Greek, to which I was in no condition to retaliate. Foreign drivers were all the same : they drove too fast, strayed on to the wrong side of the road, never paid attention, were often drunk. Greek friends later explained to me that this shrill tirade was motivated not by heartlessness but by the paramount need to establish her son's innocence in the affair as quickly as possible. She had assumed – rightly, as it turned out – that the police would take the side of some seemingly wealthy and influential foreigners rather than that of a semi-literate peasant transporting from one village to another some timber and the womenfolk who had played the major part in its collection.

Unhurt, Alethea Hayter and Brian de Jongh behaved with impeccable coolness and resource and in no time at all they had flagged down a huge American station-wagon. By then I was able not merely to climb into its rear but to help to heave Maurice aboard. Our driver – ashen, clutching his side (we learned later that he had broken a number of ribs) but stoically uncomplaining – also joined us. Alethea and Brian decided to wait with the driver, his lamenting or upbraiding womenfolk and the group of gesticulating and shouting peasants who had materialised from nowhere. until the police arrived.

'You all right?' the American owners of the station-wagon would from time to time peer round to ask us. Middle-aged husband and wife, what was really worrying them was not whether we were all right but whether the upholstery of their car was all right. They had already spread sheets of the *Athens News* and the *New York Herald Tribune* for us to bleed on to. Maurice, conscious now but dazed, for once was silent when asked a question, his head lolling from side to side as we lurched round one hairpin bend after another. It was left to me to answer; and suddenly – no doubt as the result of the excess of adrenalin that the shock of the accident must have sent pumping through my system – I experienced an extraordinary euphoria that made me talk and talk and talk, like one of those bomb-victims of the last war who would emerge Lazarus-like from the rubble not merely smiling but chattering their heads off, to the mingled admiration and boredom of their rescuers.

'Mandra should have a doctor or at least a pharmacy,' the male American said. He had already told me that he and his wife were missionaries, to which I remember that I answered fatuously, 'How nice, how very nice.'

'The sooner you get attention, the better,' the wife said. 'I don't think it would be wise to wait until we get to Athens.' What she really meant, of course, was that the sooner we got attention, the better for that upholstery.

Her husband began to describe to me a spectacular pile-up in which they had been involved the previous summer on an *autobahn*. 'Now that really *was* a crash.' I felt fleetingly ashamed that we ourselves had not been able to do better for him.

Neither of them could speak a word of Greek, though they had been in the country for some time, and it was I who had to ask a villager in Mandra the way to the nearest doctor. After having first ascertained what nationality we were, where we had come from and what had happened to us, he eventually directed us to a 'polyclinic'.

'I hope you'll forgive us if we don't stay with you,' the wife said as we were helped out of the car. 'But you seem to be in excellent hands now.'

I never saw them again; I never learned their names.

The Greek doctor, young and handsome, in a short-sleeved white tunic that revealed arms covered in a dark fuzz, placed the fingers of each hand on either side of my nose and clicked it painfully from side to side, so that a few drops of blood trickled out of it. He shook his head, seemingly disappointed. 'Not broken,' he said in Greek.

Maurice, dazed and still silent, was now half-coaxed and half-hoisted on to a couch by two giggling peasant-girls in the uniforms of nurses, after they had first removed his jacket, shirt and tie. The Greek pressed and tapped his supine torso; took out his stethoscope and listened intently, while the two girls continued to giggle behind him; felt Maurice's pulse. Then he ordered the two girls to remove Maurice's trousers. They shook their heads vehemently; backed away as though from something contaminated and contaminating; covered their faces with their hands, the cheeks behind them crimson. The doctor shouted angrily at them and, themselves angry now, they shouted back at him.

I resolved the altercation by myself undoing the buttons of the trousers strained tight across that ample belly. The girls consented to remove the shoes. Then I began to tug at the trouser-ends. What was eventually revealed, after considerable effort, in the centre of a swelling mass of blubber was a Delphi in microcosm. The girls averted their eyes, the doctor once more tapped and palpated. With the same disappointment with which he had told me that my nose was not broken, he finally announced that there were no internal injuries. He would merely have to stitch up a cut above an eyebrow. What neither of us realised was that the driver, seated unbloodied and stoical on a straight-backed kitchen-type chair while awaiting his turn (my guess would be that the doctor had left him to the last out of a sense of social precedence), was the only one of us seriously hurt.

The next day, when I went to see how he was getting on, Maurice said to me: 'Yes, it was a nasty moment – a distinctly nasty moment. When I saw that bloody great juggernaut coming straight at us, I remember that my last thought was "My God, what a loss to English culture!"' My vain (in both senses) hope that Alethea and myself might perhaps have been included in that envisaged loss was dispelled when he went on: 'But I don't know really. Let's face it, my best work – the work by which I'll be remembered – has probably all been done by now.'

Later I said: 'Didn't Alethea behave magnificently? Tearing up all that underwear and using up all those handkerchiefs and never for a moment showing any sign of panic.'

'Oh, yes, yes.'

A friend who was with us put in: 'I always think it was women like that who won the war for us.'

Maurice grunted. 'And made it such hell for everyone else.'

We all laughed; and now, though I have forgotten many Bowra sallies that made me laugh more at the time of their utterance, that particular one has somehow stuck with me, partly because it still strikes me as funny but chiefly because it seems to me to epitomise one of the dominant traits of his character. I don't think that he would ever have sacrificed a friend for a material advantage; but if it was a question of sacrificing a witticism, then that was another matter. He shared, I knew, my affection and admiration for Alethea and now we both owed her a debt of gratitude; but that did not preclude a joke.

Similarly when, at Delphi, we had talked of Evelyn Waugh, Maurice's wit kept us laughing continuously. I remember particularly how, when I said that I thought that the *Men at Arms* trilogy the best thing that Waugh had done to date, Maurice had expostulated 'Oh, but you *can't* believe that! I always call it "The Waugh to end Waugh".' There is also that story, perhaps apocryphal, of Maurice's decision to get married. When he announced that he had at last chosen a girl, a friend remonstrated: 'But you can't marry anyone as plain as that.' Maurice answered: 'My dear fellow, buggers can't be choosers.'

After our Delphi adventure, I used to see him intermittently during my visits to England, although we were never again to achieve that same intimacy as when I removed his trousers. Once in Japan I was approached by a professor of English, about to visit Britain for the first time in his life, with the request that I should give him a letter of introduction to 'Sir Bowra' – whom apparently he admired more than any other living English scholar. Since the Japanese was virtually incapable of speaking a word of English, even though he could write it impeccably, I found myself in a quandary. I could hardly tell a man who was head of the English faculty of one of the most prestigious of Japanese universities that his English was not good enough for me to help him; but at the same time I shrank from inflicting someone so tedious on Maurice. Eventually I wrote the introduction. Some weeks later, a letter arrived from Wadham – 'Thank you so much for sending me your Professor X. We had a long and interesting silence together. He rewarded me with a doll . . .'

I think that even if our days together in Greece had not had as their climax that disaster on the road from Delphi, they would none the less remain vivid in my mind. A constant source of tribulation to me in my British Council days was the acute boredom that I experience when I have to listen to a lecture either by others or by myself. But I could hear Maurice deliver the same lecture twice or even three times with no diminution of pleasure at the bravura of his performance: I have never met anyone who could talk more entertainingly when in form. But more than all this was his ability to *notice*. Like Raymond Mortimer when he came on a visit to Kyoto, Maurice made me see things on our visit to Delphi of which, in the course of many visits there with people of hardly less eminence, I had been totally unaware. Often what he pointed out was trivial – the beauty of some olive-tree against crumbling masonry, the early morning sunlight on the roof of our hotel, the fact that the main gate to the sanctuary of Pythian Apollo was preceded by five steps to make it impossible for anyone to drive up to the temple in a chariot – but what he told me then still remains with me, so that whenever I return to Delphi, he seems uncannily to be beside me.

17

John Bowle

A Plain Way with Heroic Poetry

* With apologies to the Shade of C.M.B.

The aim of heroic poetry is to excite, to shock and to stun. In conversation some of us can do this, but the bard is confined to traditional idioms and to the clichés that enlarge them. 'We had a bumpy flight; C was sick and K could not eat his caviare' describes succinctly what it is meant to describe. The bard must say 'After rosy-fingered dawn had lit the mountains, Proteus, master of wind and storm, enveloped their chariot in a cloud; C, lover of the wine cup, cast up his account to Dionysus, and K, lover of long-backed sturgeons, rejected even the food of the Gods.' Heroic poetry from Gilgamesh to Beowulf and the Elder Edda buys its elevation at a price, and we must interpret it in a plain way.

Classical prose writers are more compact. A modern writer might elaborate the episode. 'Told to tighten his seat belt, C (so subjective and introspective) felt that he had nothing to put it round: while K, all appetite for living extinguished, remarked (for it was a French aeroplane), *Je m'en fiche de tout ça.*' Thucydides would have briefly pointed the moral: 'Thus these gadabouts had their own reward, seeing that the one had neglected virtue, and the other given himself over to Ionian luxury.' Tacitus would have been even more laconic: 'Stability being absent, hope was lost.'

Anglo-Saxon prose is more devious. It was often composed in riddles. The audience was first excited by the question, then stunned by the explanation, though seldom shocked by it. Our theme, translated, becomes: 'High in heaven's pathways I fly above the earth. Yet dread I the mists of Grendel over the marsh. I hold inside me mighty thanes, but their insides are empty. Far below the swan-way receives its ransom. Who (or what) am I?'

If we leave this brisk conundrum, with its insight into the Dark Ages, and turn to Chaucer, we find that he is more factual.

> '*Although by Goddes' helpe saafe and sounde*
> *Yet hadde we cause enuff to sweate and swounde,*
> *So fearsome was ye rockinge of ye playne*
> *Thatt feared we never to come hoome agayne.*
> *And C, a woorthie likerish and fatte,*
> *Eftsoones incontinent begonne to catte;*
> *While K, y-belted cloose withyn his seate,*
> *Could neither take hys drinke or eke his meate.*'

Marlowe, of course, has greater attack.

> '*Now that the pouerfull maister of the skie*
> *Assailled by gloomie tempests as it flies,*
> *Dips and ascends through dizzy heights of aire,*
> *Olde C his sinnes come welling up apace,*
> *And K spurnes tribute from far Caspian.*'

Thus a commonplace but poignant episode can be interpreted in different ways – mysterious, realistic and romantic. Baudelaire might have described it admirably, or Rimbaud with his even wider experience of disorientation. One recalls the former's *Comme sur les vagues du Sud l'albatrosse s'ennuie,* or the latter's *Quand sur la mer de glace je me trouve glisser.*

Greek dramatists chose nobler themes, and the technique of dramatic verse is more subtle. We are left to use our own imaginations. Where Aeschylus describes Hercules' feeling for Hylas and his grief at the boy's fate, the situation speaks all too clearly for itself. There is not, and had better not be, any more to be said. The fears of Ganymede in the Eagle's grip become insignificant to us when we imagine the joys that await him in the lap of the Gods. Where Oedipus is burnt alive, we feel it right that this should happen off stage; and children being what they are, the grief of Hecuba for hers is the more poignant to us if we have not set eyes on them.

Greek sculptors tried to embody an ideal of perfect manhood. The sturdy 'Boxer of Rhodes' shows one obvious aspect of it, and the 'Gymnast of Poros' several others. But we may well believe the tale of the painter Meretrikos, who, asked why he made some portraits more flattering than others, replied 'Handsome is as handsome pays'.

Greek wine cups and amphorae are often anecdotal. There is a moving vase from Kos which represents an orgy on one side and the hangover after it on the other; and the Greeks did not shrink from depicting the more intimate aspects of love in all their variety; as in the celebrated Demi-Vierges at Play from Lesbos, the Apollo with Boy-friend from Delos or the well-known Satyr with Goat in the Vatican. In our own country the Bayeux tapestry, undoubtedly Anglo-Saxon work, has a similar realism, and its borders do not shirk the aftermath of battle in the field or the bedroom. Medieval illuminators, too, when they depict a battle, make no more bones about it than those already there, and if some Elizabethan portraits look wooden it may well be because their subjects were blockheads. Like the best critics of literature, these artists seldom left the ground and are the better for it.

So the poets, dramatists and artists of Hellas and of Anglo-Saxon, Chaucerian and Elizabethan England, described the human condition in contrasting ways. We can make what we like or dislike of them; but they have to be reckoned with. Nor ought we to neglect the fragments we possess of the Cradle Songs of the Eskimos, crooned in the intimate acoustics of their igloos, or the haunting chants of the more primitive Australians, howled in their corroborees. The initiation rites of the Trobriand Islanders were accompanied by memorable incantations, and crude though the rhythms may sometimes appear, they express directly the pains, and the pleasures, of those concerned. In primitive song the more elemental passions are unconcealed. Though more recondite and compassionate feelings may appeal to us, the Shaman and the Witchdoctor knew what they were up to and down to. The rhythmic choruses of Viti Levu were stamped out round the cooking pot as an enemy or a missionary was done to a turn, and they can still appeal to all of us who enjoy the culinary art.

Thus we conclude that the human spirit is manifest in different ways, and that in all its various forms we should respect and understand it.

18

John Sparrow

C.M.B.

Which of the two, when God and Maurice meet,
Will occupy – you ask – the judgment seat?
Sure, our old friend – each one of us replies –
Will justly dominate the Grand Assize:
He'll seize the sceptre and annex the throne,
Claim the Almighty's thunder for his own,
Trump the Last Trump, and the Last Post postpone.
Then, if his strong prerogative extends
To passing sentence on his sinful friends,
Thus shall we supplicate at Heaven's high bar:
'Be merciful! you made us what we are;
Our jokes, our joys, our hopes, our hatreds too,
The outrageous things we do, or want to do –
How much of all of them we owe to you!
Send us to Hell or Heaven or where you will,
Promise us only, you'll be with us still:
Without you, Heaven would be too dull to bear,
And Hell will not be Hell if you are there.'

* Published in the *Times Literay Supplement* on 23 June 1972

Contributors

Lord Annan is Provost of University College, London, and was formerly Provost of King's College, Cambridge.

Sir Isaiah Berlin OM is President of Wolfson College, Oxford.

Sir John Betjeman is Poet Laureate.

John Bowle is an historian.

Cyril Connolly is a writer and critic, and was founder and editor of *Horizon*.

John H. Finley, Jr. is Professor of Greek at Harvard.

Susan Gardiner lives in Oxford, and is married to the philosopher P. L. Gardiner.

Francis King is a novelist.

Osbert Lancaster is a writer and cartoonist.

Hugh Lloyd-Jones is Regius Professor of Greek at Oxford.

Leslie Mitchell is an historian and a Fellow of University College, Oxford.

Mercurius Oxoniensis is a pseudonymous writer in the *Spectator*.

Anthony Powell is a novelist.

Anthony Quinton is a philosopher and a Fellow of New College, Oxford.

John Sparrow is Warden of All Souls College, Oxford.

Sir Kenneth Wheare was formerly Vice-Chancellor of Oxford University and Rector of Exeter College.

Sir Mortimer Wheeler CH is an archaeologist, and was formerly Honorary Secretary of the British Academy.

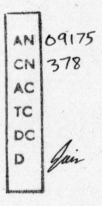